ECCLESIASTES

The Hodder Bible Commentary

Edited by Lee Gatiss

ECCLESIASTES

ERIC ORTLUND

HODDER &
STOUGHTON

The Hodder Bible Commentary
Series Editor: Lee Gatiss

First published in Great Britain in 2024 by Hodder & Stoughton
An Hachette UK company

1

The Hodder Bible Commentary: Ecclesiastes copyright © Eric Ortlund 2024

The right of Eric Ortlund to be identified as the Author of the Work has been asserted
by him in accordance with the Copyright, Designs and Patents Act 1988.

Unless otherwise indicated, scripture quotations are taken from
Holy Bible, New International Version® (Anglicised), NIV™
Copyright © 1979, 1984, 2011 by Biblica Inc. Published by Hodder & Stoughton Ltd.
Used with permission. All rights reserved worldwide.
'NIV' is a registered trademark of Biblica Inc.
UK trademark number 1448790.

Scripture quotations marked (ESV) are taken from The ESV® Bible (The Holy Bible, English
Standard Version®), copyright © 2001 by Crossway, a publishing ministry of
Good News Publishers. Used by permission. All rights reserved.

Surprised By Joy by C. S. Lewis © copyright 1955 CS Lewis Pte Ltd.
Extract used with permission.

All rights reserved. No part of this publication may be reproduced, stored in a retrieval system, or
transmitted, in any form or by any means without the prior written permission of the publisher,
nor be otherwise circulated in any form of binding or cover other than that in which it is
published and without a similar condition being imposed on the subsequent purchaser.

A CIP catalogue record for this title is available from the British Library

Hardback ISBN 9781529302110
ebook ISBN 9781473695207

Typeset in Bembo Std and Utopia by Palimpsest Book Production Ltd, Falkirk, Stirlingshire

Printed and bound in Great Britain by Clays Ltd, Elcograf S.p.A.

Hodder & Stoughton policy is to use papers that are natural, renewable and recyclable products
and made from wood grown in sustainable forests. The logging and manufacturing processes
are expected to conform to the environmental regulations of the country of origin.

Hodder & Stoughton Ltd
Carmelite House
50 Victoria Embankment
London EC4Y 0DZ

www.hodderfaith.com
www.hodderbiblecommentary.com

Contents

Series Preface	xi
Consultant Editors	xiii
Acknowledgements	xiv
Author's Preface	xv
Abbreviations	xvii
Hebrew Words Frequently Used	xviii
Introduction	1
1 Introduction and Main Thesis: Vanity of Vanities! (Ecclesiastes 1:1–11)	25
2 Qoholet's Autobiography: Three Investigations (Ecclesiastes 1:12–2:26)	49
3 Everything Beautiful in Its Time (Ecclesiastes 3:1–15)	73
4 Oppression (Ecclesiastes 3:16–22)	85
5 Five 'Better-than' Statements (Ecclesiastes 4)	91
6 True Piety (Ecclesiastes 5:1–7)	97
7 Wealth and Its Enjoyment (Ecclesiastes 5:8–6:9)	103
8 What Is Really Good? (Ecclesiastes 6:10–7:14)	111

9	Righteousness and Wisdom Subject to Vanity *(Ecclesiastes 7:15–29)*	*123*
10	Acting Wisely Before the King *(Ecclesiastes 8:1–9)*	*133*
11	The Problem of Delayed Judgment *(Ecclesiastes 8:10–17)*	*139*
12	Death as a Catalyst to Joy *(Ecclesiastes 9)*	*147*
13	Various Proverbs *(Ecclesiastes 10)*	*157*
14	Generous Work Before a Cosmic Funeral *(Ecclesiastes 11:1–12:8)*	*165*
15	Words of Delight: Editor's Conclusion *(Ecclesiastes 12:9–14)*	*183*

The life of mortals is like grass,
they flourish like a flower of the field;
the wind blows over it and it is gone,
and its place remembers it no more.
(Psalm 103:15–16)

I have held many things in my hands, and
I have lost them all; but whatever I have placed
in God's hands, that I still possess.
(Martin Luther)

Dedication

This book is dedicated to my dear daughter, Kate, in the hope that its wisdom and its joy will be hers.

Series Preface

The unfolding of your words gives light
(Psalm 119:130)

The Hodder Bible Commentary aims to proclaim afresh in our generation the unchanging and unerring word of God, for the glory of God and the good of his people. This fifty-volume commentary on the whole Bible seeks to provide the contemporary church with fresh and readable expositions of Scripture which are doctrinally sensitive and globally aware, accessible for all adult readers but particularly useful to those who preach, teach and lead Bible studies in churches and small groups.

Building on the success of Hodder's NIV Proclamation Bible, we have assembled as contributors a remarkable team of men and women from around the world. Alongside a diverse panel of trusted Consultant Editors, they have a tremendous variety of denominational backgrounds and ministries. Each has great experience in unfolding the gospel of Jesus Christ and all are united in our aim of faithfully expounding the Bible in a way that takes account of the original text, biblical theology, the history of interpretation and the needs of the contemporary global church.

These volumes are serious expositions – not overly technical, scholarly works of reference but not simply sermons either. As well as carefully unpacking what the Bible says, they are sensitive to how it has been used in doctrinal discussions over the centuries and in our own day, though not dominated by such concerns at the expense of the text's own agenda. They also try to speak not only into a white, middle-class, Western context (for example), as some might, but to be aware of ways in which other cultures hear and need to hear what the Spirit is saying to the churches.

As you tuck into his word, with the help of this book, may the glorious Father 'give you the Spirit of wisdom and revelation, so that you may know him better' (Ephesians 1:17).

Lee Gatiss, Series Editor

Consultant Editors

The Series Editor would like to thank the following Consultant Editors for their contributions to the Hodder Bible Commentary:

Shady Anis (*Egypt*)
Kirsten Birkett (*UK*)
Felipe Chamy (*Chile*)
Ben Cooper (*UK*)
Mervyn Eloff (*South Africa*)
Keri Folmar (*Dubai*)
Kerry Gatiss (*UK*)
Kara Hartley (*Australia*)
Julian Hardyman (*Madagascar*)
Stephen Fagbemi (*Nigeria*)
Rosanne Jones (*Japan*)
Henry Jansma (*USA*)
Samuel Lago (*USA*)
Andis Miezitis (*Latvia*)
Adrian Reynolds (*UK*)
Peter Ryan (*Australia*)
Sookgoo Shin (*South Korea*)
Myrto Theocharous (*Greece*)

Acknowledgements

My friends and comrades in Christ, Anne Andrews and Steve Walsh, both read this book in manuscript form and made many helpful comments. The book is better for their work and I am deeply grateful to them both.

As always, I find no adequate words for my lovely wife, Erin, except that your encouragement and grace mean the world to me, and this book would be much the worse without you.

Author's Preface

Thank you for picking up this book. I did not write it to waste your time. I wrote it because I love the book of Ecclesiastes and I want you to love it too – and the God who inspired it.

I love Ecclesiastes because it saved my ministry (and probably my sanity). If it hadn't been for this troubling and joyful book, I may very well have given up on God's path for my life. This is a commentary and not an autobiography, but the main reason I find Ecclesiastes so helpful is that it diagnoses our tendency to link the value of our work (and our self-worth) with visible and measurable results: my life matters because I'm making a difference in the world. Ecclesiastes does not deny that we have an impact, but it does ask us to face up to the hard truth that, from a this-worldly, 'under the sun' perspective, we are soon in the grave and whatever mark we made is wiped away (our place 'remembers [us] no more', as in Psalm 103:16). In light of this, Ecclesiastes wants to sever the link between the value of our lives and what we accomplish and instead link it with God's goodness. Your life under the sun matters not according to what you'll accomplish – because, under the sun, you accomplish nothing permanent. Your life matters because God has given you a gift called 'today', to work in and to enjoy. Your life and your work are valuable because God has directly given them to you, not because of whatever kind of impact you will have.

I believe this wisdom is highly counter-intuitive, under-appreciated in our context and deeply helpful, both for engaging wisely with our deeply good and deeply frustrating existence 'under the sun', and for enduring with joy until that day when the sun falls from the heavens (2 Peter 3:10) and we receive that final reward of which we gain only hints in our earthly lives (Matthew 25:21).

Abbreviations

BDB	Francis Brown, S. R. Driver and Charles Briggs, *A Hebrew and English Lexicon of the Old Testament* (Peabody: Hendrickson, 1996)
GKC	Wilhelm Gesenius and E. Kautzsch, *Gesenius' Hebrew Grammar* (Oxford: Clarendon, 1910)
HALOT	Ludwig Köehler and Walter Baumgartner, *The Hebrew and Aramaic Lexicon of the Old Testament* (Leiden: Brill, 2001)
WOC	Bruce Waltke and Michael O'Connor, *An Introduction to Biblical Hebrew Syntax* (Winona Lake: Eisenbrauns, 1990)

Hebrew Words Frequently Used

Qohelet The Hebrew word appropriately translated as 'the Teacher' in 1:1, 7:27 and 12:9. Although not a proper name, I use the word as a name for the teacher in Ecclesiastes.

hebel Qohelet's favourite word for describing life under the sun, translated as 'meaningless' by the NIV, but I think better translated as 'brevity' or 'vanity'. It is hard to find one English word that encompasses all the ways it is used in Ecclesiastes.

yitron Permanent gain or profit – which Qohelet thinks no one gets under the sun.

Introduction

Let's begin our exploration of Ecclesiastes by reflecting on two different kinds of experiences which most people undergo repeatedly throughout their lives. Although it will not be immediately obvious, doing so will put us in a strong position to appreciate what this troubling and beautiful book has to say to us.

You are about halfway through another morning at work. It is another Tuesday among hundreds you've worked through, looking at a screen, typing. You are utterly submerged within the day, hardly even aware of yourself, hardly tasting the coffee at your desk. Then, without warning, something draws your attention to yourself and your surroundings in an unexpectedly intense way. Perhaps you look outside and see the sun shining through the clouds, and you are struck by its beauty, the sheer *thereness* of it, and feel simply glad you are alive to see it. Perhaps you hear music from your teenage years, and for just a second you remember what it felt like to be young, and what music sounded like then. Perhaps you receive unexpected bad news which makes you suddenly grateful for the job and home and health you had hardly even noticed before. Whatever the cause, you are jolted awake; nothing changes externally, but a kind of brilliance rests on everything for just a moment. But eventually you have to get back to work – and by the afternoon, you can hardly remember what it felt like to view the world with such startled attention. You sink into the ordinariness of life and are submerged once more. Perhaps years pass before you are jolted awake again; but the experience never quite leaves you, perforating the days and years as they pass, as if some magnificent secret were just about to be revealed – but always, always it eludes you, as life grinds on.

Moments of awe like this are a blessing, but a very different kind of experience meets most of us with similar intensity. Sometimes it is not the beauty of ordinary things which grips us but total frustration with them, and something inside, stubborn as a donkey, simply refuses to carry on for a moment or two. The external causes vary: perhaps you were faced again, for the thousandth time, with the blind spots or failures of a spouse or family member; perhaps you have to own up to the fact that you will never get your business to be profitable, no matter how many hours you sink into it; perhaps you read another horrifying headline of some injustice perpetrated at home or around the world, and wonder what is wrong with the human race for the most vulnerable human beings to be treated so brutally. And for a moment, something inside refuses all of creation. If the world were to blip out of existence, it would feel like a relief. Why should the world continue to grind on? How can all the grind and waste be worth it? You have no answer.

I trust I'm not the only one who has found himself in both of these situations repeatedly. One doesn't so much seek them out as find oneself confronted by them, for good or bad. It is worth reflecting how we could react to life in such opposite ways – finding the same existence at times too beautiful for words, at other times intolerably frustrating. And am I the only one who has wondered if there was a way to hold onto the beauty and preciousness of the most ordinary things, without becoming submerged and forgetful in yet another Tuesday morning? And what if there was a way to receive the preciousness of the ordinary, without ignoring the frustrating and ugly sides of life after the fall?

INTRODUCTION

The ancient book of Ecclesiastes gives wisdom about how to do exactly this, in a way unlike any I have ever read, inside the Bible or outside of it. Getting at this wisdom will not be easy or quick. The book has many difficult things to say to us (12:11). But I have found the journey repays itself many times over.

To receive the precious wisdom that Ecclesiastes offers, however, we will have to start with some very ordinary questions: who wrote it, when and for whom; how the book has been read by others, both in the past and in our own age; how we can read it well; and how it fits with the rest of the Bible.

1. *Author, date, original context*

Although biblical books are not limited to their original context, it is helpful to know, for example, about the well-meaning but corrupting legalism that sparked Paul's letter to the Galatians, or that the Song of Songs is meant to help Israelite teenagers wisely negotiate the beautiful, sometimes-painful, experience of falling in love and getting married. When we ask questions about the original author and date of Ecclesiastes, however, things get complicated. (I summarise here a longer argument made in the commentary on 1:1 – see below for details.)

First, there are not one but two distinct voices in the book. The first is that of the Teacher, mentioned in 1:1, 7:27 and 12:9. The word translated 'Teacher' is *qōhelet*, which is not a name but a job title (he is called 'the Qohelet' in 7:27, 12:9); I find it nevertheless helpful to refer to the Teacher as 'Qohelet' when talking about Ecclesiastes. A second anonymous voice talks about the Teacher Qohelet in the third person, recommending his wisdom to us (12:9–10) with something of a caution (verses 11–12).

Since this Teacher is a son of David ruling over all Israel (1:1, 12), many have naturally identified Qohelet with Solomon. Although I certainly would not insist on the issue, I think it is better (for reasons developed below) to take the Qohelet as a literary persona created by an anonymous Israelite sage. Were Solomon the author, there would be no reason for him not to be named directly, nor would there be any reason for a later author to recommend to us a writing from Israel's wisest king. On the other hand, if an author wanted to engage us in a thought experiment, it would make sense for him to evoke a Solomon-like persona without naming him. This allows the anonymous author to communicate certain uncomfortable truths we might otherwise find easy to dismiss.[1] It is a way of saying, 'Imagine someone of Solomon-like authority, resources and ability. He can do anything he wants in life. Surely, if anyone could be happy, it would be him, right? But he was actually one of the most depressed people ever – until he learned how to engage with life in a very different way.'

Just as the framing author who passes on Qohelet's words is anonymous, so he does not give us any clear indication about when he wrote. I argue below that there are some indications it was written in the post-exilic period of Israel's history, but it is impossible to be more specific. Nor does there seem to be any particular event or problem that sparked his writing. The very nature of the book makes it broadly relevant to the members of every generation who live out their lives 'under the sun'.

Although there is no specific situation that the book addresses, the genre does help us understand its intentions and goals. Ecclesiastes is wisdom literature, to be read alongside Proverbs, Job

---

[1] The practice of otherwise unknown editors passing on wisdom teaching by adding some introductory and closing comments of their own was not uncommon in the ancient world. Michael Fox lists a number of other examples in *A Time to Tear Down and a Time to Build Up: A Rereading of Ecclesiastes* (Grand Rapids: Eerdmans, 1999), 367–70. He also discusses different possibilities for relating the book's two voices and argues in a way I find convincing that we should see a single author standing behind both voices in the book (see 363–6).

and the Song of Songs. We know this because (like those other books) there are very few references to the Exodus, covenant, Law, Temple and Promised Land which so occupy Genesis to Kings and the Prophets. Instead, there is a focus on what patterns God has instituted in creation and how we can live skilfully within them. There are also a number of echoes in vocabulary among these books, such as the word 'wisdom' itself (*ḥākam* and *hokmāh*). The reference to 'my son' in 12:12 recalls the same in Proverbs 1–9, where the father passes on insight about how to live wisely and blessedly within the complex patterns God has set up in his world. Ecclesiastes has the same perspective and intention – but also has unique insights about how God disposes of the present order of the world.

2. How has Ecclesiastes been read in the past?

2 Timothy 3:16–17 has rightly been cherished as one of the most significant statements of the divine inspiration and authority of Scripture. What is less often noticed is the reference in verse 14 to those who taught Timothy the Bible. What was true for Paul's son in the faith is true for every believer – each of us is indebted to other teachers of God's word, some known to us personally, and some whom we have never met, but only read. We each learn the Scriptures with much help from others. Tracing some of the ways in which Ecclesiastes has been read by earlier generations can help us understand the book today – even when (and especially when) they did not quite get it right. One can learn much even from mistakes.

Roland Murphy lays out three basic assumptions about how Christians read Ecclesiastes up until the Reformation: it was authored by Solomon; statements about vanity or the meaninglessness of life are to be interpreted against the perspective of eternity and the next life; and tensions in the book mean that

Solomon is dialoguing with sceptics, i.e., difficult verses are to be attributed to a third party with whom Solomon disagrees.[2] One example of this is found in St. Gregory Thaumaturgus's *Metaphrase of Ecclesiastes* (circa 210–60). He summarises Ecclesiastes 1:2–3 in the following way:

> How vain and fruitless are the affairs of men, and all pursuits that occupy man! For there is not one who can tell of any profit attaching to those things which men who creep on earth strive by body and soul to attain to, in servitude all the while to what is transient, and undesirous of considering anything heavenly with the noble eye of the soul.[3]

In other words, Ecclesiastes is meant to provoke us to contemplate unchanging spiritual truths which, in comparison to the vanity of earthly things, are of great profit.[4] Jerome (347–420) makes exactly the same move. For example, he asks why Ecclesiastes describes 'vanity of vanities' if everything God made is very good (Genesis 1:31).[5] His answer: although the world is good in itself, in comparison to God it is only vanity, like a candle next to the sun. This kind of approach to Ecclesiastes, emphasising contempt

---

[2] Roland Murphy, 'Qohelet Interpreted: The Bearing of the Past on the Present', *Vetus Testamentum* 32 (1982): 331–2. For those interested in this history of interpretation of Ecclesiastes, see Michael Fox, 'Qohelet', *Dictionary of Biblical Interpretation*, ed. John Hayes (Nashville: Abingdon, 1999), 2:346–54; Tremper Longman, 'Ecclesiastes 3: History of Interpretation', *Dictionary of the Old Testament: Wisdom, Poetry and Writings*, eds. Tremper Longman and Peter Enns (Downers Grove: IVP Academic, 2008), 140–49; Christian Ginsburg, *Coheleth* (London: Longman, Green, Longman and Roberts, 1861), 27–253.

[3] See John Jarick, *Gregory Thaumaturgos' Paraphrase of Ecclesiastes* (Atlanta: Scholars, 1990), 7–9.

[4] See further Craig Bartholomew, *Ecclesiastes* (Grand Rapids: Baker, 2009), 26.

[5] Jerome, *Commentary on Ecclesiastes*, trans. Richard Goodrich and David Miller (New York: Newman, 2012), 35–6.

INTRODUCTION

for the world in comparison to eternity, would be extremely influential for the next thousand years.

Early Christians also found their way around seemingly difficult statements in the book by attributing them to sceptics. For example, Gregory says that Ecclesiastes 9:1–3 are words spoken by a fool.[6] He is even bolder with regard to 2:16, with which he flatly disagrees, saying, 'There is nothing common to the wise and to the fool, whether it be human memory or God's reward.' Only a fool would talk that way![7]

We will see below that some modern commentators have a similar struggle: it is easy to read certain verses and think, 'The Bible can't possibly be saying that.' Nevertheless, Ecclesiastes itself never clearly separates any of its statements as representing an opposite or foolish point of view. Furthermore, the Teacher Qohelet's response to the vanity or brevity of this world is the opposite of that of early Christians: instead of pointing to the great value of eternal things, he recommends full enjoyment of temporal things. We will consider this further below.

The Jewish rabbis interpreted Ecclesiastes in a somewhat similar way, but gave much more attention to integrating the book with obedience to Torah. Touching down at two points in the thousands of pages of rabbinic literature will be instructive.

First, the Great Midrash (compiled around the thirteenth century) comments on Ecclesiastes 1:3 by saying that the book is saved from heresy in three ways. The first is the reminders of divine judgment, which set appropriate boundaries to the call to enjoy life. Second, the 'under the sun' perspective limits the book's statements to this life, leaving the life of the world to

---

[6] Jarick, *Gregory Thaumaturgus' Paraphrase*, 226.

[7] Jarick, *Gregory Thaumaturgus' Paraphrase*, 43. See further a number of helpful quotations from the church fathers in *Ancient Christian Commentary on Scripture: Proverbs, Ecclesiastes, Song of Solomon*, ed. J. Robert Wright (Old Testament 9; Downers Grove: InterVarsity Press, 2005), 190–201.

come free from vanity. Third, when Ecclesiastes 1:3 says that all labour is without profit, this refers to one's occupation, not to the study of Torah, which does profit in this life.[8] This provided a way for early Jewish readers to integrate Ecclesiastes with the rest of their Bibles. (As we will see below, I believe the second point is insightful, but the third is wrong.)

The Targum of Ecclesiastes (probably written sometime after the fifth century) shows a similar attempt to fit the book in with the rest of the Hebrew Bible by reading it in relation to King Solomon and the history of Israel.[9] This is how Ecclesiastes 1:1–4 is rendered (the italicised words are those added by the Aramaic translator):

> The words of *prophecy* which Qohelet, *that is, Solomon* the son of David the king who was in Jerusalem, *prophesied*. (2) *When Solomon King of Israel saw through the holy spirit that the kingdom of Rehoboam his son would be divided with Jeroboam the son of Nebat and that Jerusalem and the Temple would be destroyed and the people of the household of Israel would go into exile,* he said *to himself*, 'Vanity of vanities *is this world*. Vanity of vanities of everything *for which I and David my father laboured*. All of it is vanity. (3) What profit does a man *have after he dies from* all his labour which he labours under the sun *in this world unless he occupies himself with Torah in order to receive a complete reward in the world to come before the Master of the world.* (4) *King Solomon said through the spirit of prophecy,* 'The good generation *of righteous ones* departs *from*

---

[8] H. Freedman and Maurice Simon (eds.), *The Midrash Rabbah: Volume 4, Lamentations; Ruth; Ecclesiastes; Song of Songs* (London: Soncino, 1977), 6–7.

[9] Targums were Aramaic translations of the Old Testament for Jewish audiences who were losing touch with Hebrew. Early Targums tend to be very literal and stick close to the original; later ones add whole paragraphs. The Targum of Ecclesiastes belongs in the second category. See Peter Knobel, *The Targum of Qohelet* (Collegeville: Liturgical Press, 1991).

the world because of the sins of the evil generation of wicked ones who will come after them.'[10]

Note how the claim to vanity is read not as referring to the nature of life under the sun as a whole, but as describing a part of the history of Israel: all things are vain with regard to David and Solomon's attempt to establish God's kingdom. The translator also neatly separates Torah study from vanity (verse 3)[11] and conveniently excuses the generation of the righteous (verse 4) from the brevity and futility which Ecclesiastes 1:1–11 describes because they died as a result of the sins of others, not because God ordains all humanity to brief lives. In the hands of the Targum translator, Ecclesiastes becomes a vehicle to teach the importance of Torah study and the reward for good works; the negative things that the book says apply either to specific parts of Israel's history or to people who disobey God. I will argue in different places below that this neatly reverses what Ecclesiastes actually wants to say. Yet the temptation to allow Ecclesiastes some validity for others – but to excuse yourself from it because you have a good relationship with God – is persistent (you may have felt it yourself as you have read the book).

We should make one more stop before turning to modern interpretations. As he did in so many other ways, Martin Luther (1483–1546) broke with tradition by interpreting Ecclesiastes as

---

[10] Knobel, *Targum of Qohelet,* 15.

[11] The Targum makes this kind of move repeatedly. For example, it translates 2:10–11 to have Solomon say that he did not withhold from himself all the joy of studying Torah, so that he might have a reward in the life of the world to come. Later Rabbis followed suit. For example, the great Jewish exegete Rashi interpreted 1:9 to mean that any learning outside Torah becomes repetitive, but Torah constantly gives new insights; see *Miqra'ot Gedolot HaKeter: Hamesh Megillot,* ed. Menahem Cohen (Tel-Aviv: Bar Ilan University, 2012), 128.

teaching engagement with the world instead of contempt for it.[12] Luther summarised the book this way: 'Solomon wants to put us at peace and to give us a quiet mind in the everyday affairs and business of this life, so that we live contentedly in the present without care and yearning about the future.'[13] Although Luther is clear that the book teaches that 'the efforts and endeavors of men are vain and useless', he nevertheless insists this does not mean Ecclesiastes teaches that ordinary life is bad (along with government, money, marriage and so on). Rather, what is condemned is the 'depraved affection' of human beings, who 'are not content with the creatures of God that we have and with their use but are always anxious and concerned to accumulate riches, honors, glory, and fame, as though we were going to live here forever'.[14] In other words, the book diagnoses the foolish way in which humanity, driven by 'foolish affections', both strives for what it does not have and fails to enjoy what it does have.[15]

For Luther, then, Ecclesiastes is meant to help us be at peace in the world without worrying about the future. Robert Kolb and Charles Arand summarise Luther's reading of Qohelet in this way:

> Lacking faith, human beings want to plan and control events and things in order to obtain the results they want. They want to define success and how to obtain it . . . Luther recognized that the human need to manage, to be in control of our plans and actions, is so deeply ingrained within every person that it will also at times characterize the Christian . . .

---

[12] Martin Luther, 'Notes on Ecclesiastes', in *Luther's Works*, ed. Jaroslav Pelikan (St. Louis: Concordia, 1972), 15:3–187.
[13] Luther, 'Notes on Ecclesiastes', 7.
[14] Luther, 'Notes on Ecclesiastes', 7–8.
[15] Luther, 'Notes on Ecclesiastes', 10.

INTRODUCTION

As Christians carry out their responsibilities in the world, faith frees them from the bondage of caring for themselves and presiding over their own destinies. Christians no longer need to be masters of their fate . . . Faith lets God be God . . . [and] lets us be us, those who are fully human and accept our finitude and dependence on God. Luther comments on Ecclesiastes, "So [the Preacher] would teach us to let things be and to let God alone do all things over, against, and without our knowledge and advice."[16]

Luther's way of reading Ecclesiastes was very influential for later generations, and I think gets much closer to what the biblical book is actually saying.

Hopefully this survey of both the insights and the mistakes of earlier generations has set a helpful context for best hearing what Ecclesiastes has to say. Before turning to the book itself, however, I want to take stock of how it has been read in modern times. As above, even mistaken interpretations will prove instructive.

3. How has Qohelet been read in modern times?

As far as I can see, Ecclesiastes has been interpreted in basically three ways in recent times. First, some interpret the book in an entirely (or mostly) positive way. Daniel Fredericks is representative.[17] He understands the key idea in the book to be not

---

[16] Robert Kolb and Charles Arand, *The Genius of Luther's Theology: A Wittenburg Way of Thinking for the Contemporary Church* (Grand Rapids: Baker Academic, 2008), 119–20. Dietrich Bonhoeffer approaches Ecclesiastes in a similar way; see the summary and extended quotes given in James Limburg, *Encountering Ecclesiastes: A Book for our Time* (Grand Rapids: Eerdmans, 2006), 47–52.

[17] Daniel Fredericks, 'Ecclesiastes', in Daniel Fredericks and Daniel Estes, *Ecclesiastes and The Song of Songs* (Downers Grove: InterVarsity Press, 2010),

meaninglessness, but transience. Qohelet's favourite word, *hebel*, literally means 'breath' elsewhere in the Old Testament, with some related metaphorical uses. Fredericks sticks close to the idea of a 'breath' which is quickly gone, in his interpretation of the book. According to Fredericks, '*coping* with, and *thriving* within, this transient life' is the theme of the book.[18] More specifically, our transience is not an indication of our lack of importance to God or the meaninglessness of life; Ecclesiastes teaches that there is a good reward and advantage for us in life, despite the fact of our brevity.[19] In other words, life has real, if temporary, value.[20]

Even though Ecclesiastes is definitely concerned with brevity, I do not believe this is the only theme in the book, or the best way to translate the word *hebel* (see commentary below on 1:2). But more significantly, Fredericks misses the frustration of Ecclesiastes. For example, when Qohelet agonises over the apparent lack of judgment of the wicked (such as in 8:10–14) – the way in which those who are most selfish and defiant of God seem to enjoy all the blessings that other parts of the Old Testament promise to the faithful – Fredericks interprets Ecclesiastes to say that this situation is only temporary, and will be eventually rectified.[21] I don't find this convincing. Qohelet is deeply troubled by what he sees, instead of indicating relief that it will soon be over. It looks like a modern way of doing

---

17–263. Norbert Lohfink's *Qoheleth*, trans. Sean McEvenue (Minneapolis: Fortress, 2003), lands in the same place, such as when he claims the poem of 1:4–11 'praises the cosmos as glorious and eternal in this image of cyclic return' (40). This misses the weary dreariness of the passage. I think Graham Ogden's *Qoheleth* (Sheffield: JSOT, 1987), 13–15, makes a similar mistake of failing to grapple with how bleak Qohelet can be.

[18] Fredericks, 'Ecclesiastes', 21, emphasis original. Fredericks sees James 4:14 as the closest New Testament parallel to Ecclesiastes.

[19] Fredericks, 'Ecclesiastes', 22–3.

[20] Fredericks, 'Ecclesiastes', 45.

[21] Fredericks, 'Ecclesiastes', 188, 194, 197.

what the Rabbis did – integrating the book with our theological expectations in a suspiciously easy way.[22]

Some interpretations go in exactly the opposite direction, however. James Crenshaw takes the main theme of Ecclesiastes to be that life 'is pointless' and 'totally absurd'; he finds this message 'oppressive' and 'radically' different from the message of Proverbs.[23] According to Crenshaw, the book teaches that there is 'no moral order at all' in the world;[24] God remains silent, distant and unhelpful, even for pious people.[25] (One reads this sort of thing frequently in commentaries, as if Qohelet's God is very different from the God of the rest of the Old Testament.[26]) If Qohelet were consistent, he would recommend suicide; but because he 'can't welcome the destruction of personal identity', he recommends enjoyment instead.[27] This seems little more than a condemned man trying to enjoy his last meal.

Crenshaw is in little danger of minimising Qohelet's frustration

---

[22] Other examples of Fredericks arguably mishandling difficult passages in Ecclesiastes could be discussed, e.g., he takes one of the book's strongest statements about sin in 7:29 as a positive thing – that God made us to seek out many explanations for things in creation. In 7:29, 'explanations' is Fredericks' translation of the NIV's 'schemes', which is more accurate. 'Ecclesiastes', 186.

[23] James Crenshaw, *Ecclesiastes: A Commentary* (Philadelphia: Westminster, 1987), 23.

[24] Crenshaw, *Ecclesiastes*, 23.

[25] Crenshaw, *Ecclesiastes*, 24.

[26] For example, God in Ecclesiastes 'is very different from the YHWH the other biblical books depict'; he 'makes a fatalistic impression' and is 'distant and cool'; Antoon Schoors, *The Preacher Sought to Find Pleasing Words: A Study of the Language of Qoheleth, Part II: Vocabulary* (Leuven: Peeters, 2004), 110. Thomas Kruger similarly claims that the relationship between God and humanity is 'more distant than in other parts of the OT'; *Qoheleth: A Commentary*, trans. O. C. Dean (Minneapolis: Fortress, 2004), 2. I will argue at several points in this commentary that this is simply incorrect: the book teaches that God is intimately at work in every aspect of human life (see 8:16–17; 11:5–6).

[27] Crenshaw, *Ecclesiastes*, 26–7.

with the world. There are, however, obvious problems with his interpretation. For example, if life is completely meaningless, why would Qohelet recommend enjoying it with such unrestrained enthusiasm (9:7–10)? Crenshaw seems to miss Qohelet's joy in the same way that Fredericks misses his frustration. Furthermore, even if Qohelet has difficulty seeing how God's justice gets worked out under the sun, he will insist on God's good judgment of every individual (3:17) and that fearing God is worth it in the end (8:12). Crenshaw does not let these passages influence his interpretation, however; he says that statements like 3:17 seem 'remarkably out of place' in Ecclesiastes,[28] and that claims like 8:12 are either an idea Qohelet quotes only to undercut or were added by later editors.[29] This seems to repeat the mistake of earlier commentators in the opposite direction: instead of conveniently fitting Ecclesiastes into our theological expectations, Crenshaw conveniently fits it into his own negative interpretation.

Crenshaw does not write with a high view of Scripture and is untroubled by apparent contradictions between biblical books. Tremper Longman, on the other hand, has written on Ecclesiastes as a conservative evangelical, but his commentary is surprisingly close to Crenshaw's.[30] Longman believes the book teaches that life is completely meaningless and that death nullifies any advantage to wisdom or work.[31] There is no reward for being righteous.[32] When Qohelet says there is nothing better than to enjoy life (e.g., 2:24), this is 'resignation, rather than affirmation';[33] there is just nothing else to do. Statements about God's sovereignty and

---

[28] Crenshaw, *Ecclesiastes*, 27. It is, of course, only out of place in Crenshaw's reductive interpretation.

[29] Crenshaw, *Ecclesiastes*, 155.

[30] Tremper Longman III, *The Book of Ecclesiastes* (Grand Rapids: Eerdmans, 1998).

[31] Longman, *Book of Ecclesiastes*, 33–4.

[32] Longman, *Book of Ecclesiastes*, 36.

[33] Longman, *Book of Ecclesiastes*, 34. This does not sit very well with the enthusiasm of passages like Ecclesiastes 9:7–10.

gifts of life and work do not make things better for Longman; he sees Qohelet's God as 'distant, occasionally indifferent, and sometimes cruel'.[34] The calls to fear God in the book (as in 5:7) amount to cowering before a dictator.[35] As a whole, Qohelet describes the meaninglessness and despair of life outside God's redeeming love.[36]

So how did this book end up in the canon? Longman sees the book's two voices (Qohelet and the anonymous author who talks about the Teacher in 1:1; 7:27; 12:9–14) as standing in tension, such that an anonymous author is presenting Qohelet's statements as a foil with which he wants the audience to disagree.[37] According to Longman, Qohelet's teaching is like the speech of the adulterous wife in Proverbs – passed on to the son only to inoculate the son against it. The obvious problem with this is the positive things that the anonymous author says about Qohelet in 12:9–14. Longman, however, argues that the book's final passage fits his interpretation. He sees 12:9–10 – which speak of the book (literally) as 'words of delight, written uprightly, words of truth' (verse 10) – as 'somewhat complimentary but very reserved', tantamount to damning Qohelet with faint praise.[38] (Longman does not explain how 12:9–10 could have been written differently to communicate a positive evaluation of Qohelet.) That Qohelet 'searched' to find words of delight implies to Longman

---

[34] Longman, *Book of Ecclesiastes*, 35.

[35] Longman, *Book of Ecclesiastes*, 36. Longman later says the command to fear God in 12:13 is different from how Qohelet uses it; *Book of Ecclesiastes*, 282. If this is true, then 'fearing God' in Ecclesiastes means something very different from whenever the phrase is used elsewhere in the Old Testament, even though the language is identical.

[36] Longman, *Book of Ecclesiastes*, 39–40.

[37] Longman, *Book of Ecclesiastes*, 37–8. Longman compares Qohelet to the speeches of the friends in Job, which are undermined by God in the end (Job 42:7–9).

[38] Longman, *Book of Ecclesiastes*, 277.

that Qohelet tried to do this but failed.³⁹ The apparent reference to God in verse 11 does not change Longman's negative interpretation, because he understands it merely as part of the metaphor with sheep goads, not a reference to God or the divine origin of the wisdom of the book.⁴⁰

All of this seems very forced to me: the obvious way to read 12:9–14 is that the author is praising Qohelet and recommending him to us. But making things worse is Longman's mistranslation of verse 12. He takes the verse not as a warning of anything in addition to what the son has received, but as a warning about the very words the son has just read: 'Furthermore, of these, my son, be warned!' (i.e., the words in Ecclesiastes 1:2–12:8).⁴¹ Unfortunately, this is a simple mistranslation. The phrase in Hebrew (*yōtēr min*) everywhere else means 'more than these', not 'of these' (*HALOT* 404; *BDB* 452; see Esther 6:6). Longman does not give any discussion of why he translates the phrase this way, either in his footnotes to the translation or his discussion of the passage.⁴² If the phrase were ambiguous or translated in different ways elsewhere, an argument could be made for a different translation here, but the phrase is entirely consistent elsewhere. The way in which Longman mistranslates this crucial verse, without any argument justifying his translation, has the unfortunate effect of taking his interpretation of Ecclesiastes outside the realm of a normal exegetical disagreement – a common and morally neutral occurrence (Ecclesiastes is a difficult book). He gives the impression of rereading the text according to what he

---

³⁹ Longman, *Book of Ecclesiastes*, 278. Longman connects this to other passages where Qohelet says that he sought something and did not find it (e.g., 7:25–9).
⁴⁰ Longman writes that to see the shepherd here as God would be a 'startling affirmation of the divine origin of wisdom' (Longman, *Book of Ecclesiastes*, 279), but other wisdom books explicitly say wisdom comes from God (e.g., Proverbs 2:6).
⁴¹ Longman, *Book of Ecclesiastes*, 276.
⁴² Longman, *Book of Ecclesiastes*, 280–81.

wants it to mean, not what the text actually says. This is a very serious mistake. We must receive God's word as it is written, not according to our expectations.

If completely negative interpretations of Ecclesiastes are no more convincing than completely positive ones, how should we proceed? Fortunately, a third vein of modern interpretation of Ecclesiastes provides a way forward. Commentaries such as those by Michael Fox and C. L. Seow do an admirable job of capturing the 'bothness' of Ecclesiastes: Qohelet's frustration and his joy.[43] I find this kind of interpretation much more helpful in terms of what the text of Ecclesiastes actually says, and I will quote both Fox and Seow repeatedly in this book.

I think the 'bothness' of Ecclesiastes is crucial to understanding the book and our lives: earthly life is both in vain and good, frustrating and joyful. To explore this further, let's set Ecclesiastes in the context of the whole Bible by exploring three significant points of contact between Ecclesiastes and other biblical books.

4. Ecclesiastes in the canon of Scripture: three points of contact

A really helpful perspective to bring to Ecclesiastes is to see it as a kind of extended commentary on Genesis 1–11: the book amounts to wise instruction in how to live after the fall of humanity, in a world cursed by God. Ecclesiastes encourages a comparison to the early chapters of Genesis through similar language and themes: Adam as dust and returning to dust in 3:19 is strongly echoed in Ecclesiastes 12:7, and 7:29 essentially

---

[43] C. L. Seow, *Ecclesiastes* (New York: Doubleday, 1997), and Fox, *A Time to Tear Down*. At a popular level, David Gibson's *Destiny: Learning to Live by Preparing to Die* (London: IVP, 2016) takes the same approach to Ecclesiastes with (in my opinion) excellent results.

summarises humankind's creation and fall in Genesis 2–3.[44] In considering this connection, it is crucial to remember that God's curse on creation in Genesis does not mean that creation is bad. Rather, his cursing imposes limitations: the blessing and fecundity of his world is not removed, but lessened and restricted. Qohelet helps us to live wisely in God's still-good creation, within these divinely imposed limitations. Genesis 3:19 is a superb verse to keep in mind as we struggle with this book: 'By the sweat of your brow you will eat your food . . . dust you are and to dust you will return.'[45] In fact, I think a good deal of what Ecclesiastes wants to do is guard us against an over-realised eschatology – against promising ourselves too much in this life.

Another helpful connection is Romans 8:20. Qohelet does not use the language of frustration, as Paul does, but God subjecting the creation 'to frustration' seems very close to Qohelet's themes of brevity and futility. As with Genesis 3, Qohelet's main question seems to be: how can we live wisely and joyfully in such a world? Other passages in Paul connect with Ecclesiastes in a similar way, such as 2 Corinthians 4:16–18. When Paul speaks of outwardly wasting away while being renewed inwardly day by day, the

---

[44] See David Clemens, 'The Law of Sin and Death: Ecclesiastes and Genesis 1–3', *Themelios* 19, no. 1 (1994): 5–8. He also connects Qohelet's focus on human labour with Genesis 3:23, and sees in 2:4–11 a hopeless attempt to try to recreate Eden. Russell Meek sees a strong echo with Genesis 4; 'The Meaning of *hebel* in Qohelet: An Intertextual Suggestion', in *The Words of the Wise Are like Goads: Engaging Qohelet in the 21st Century*, ed. Mark Boda, Tremper Longman and Christian Rata (Winona Lake: Eisenbrauns, 2013), 241–56, especially 254. Abel's name in Hebrew is actually Qohelet's favourite and oft-repeated word *hebel*, and Abel's story illustrates many of Qohelet's frustrations: brevity, a lack of reward and injustice.

[45] A. B. Caneday justly asks if we can receive Ecclesiastes as a book that 'enhances or completes the full range of biblical orthodoxy' by showing us our true position in life under the sun, after the fall; '"Everything Is Vapor:" Grasping for Meaning Under the Sun', *Southern Baptist Journal of Theology* 15, no. 3 (2011): 27.

latter of those two realities is of course more important – that as-yet-unseen eternal weight of glory. But that does not mean our physical bodies are worthless (compare 1 Timothy 4:1–5). Although God surely wants our hopes fixed on the eternal, he has given us one book in the canon to help us live wisely in our fading bodies. Our earthly lives are still good, still worthy of attention, even if they are quickly gone.

Finally, something should be said about Ecclesiastes and Proverbs. It is not always easy to see how these two books can be in the same Bible, for the glowing promises of life, wealth, favour, success and blessing that Proverbs promises to the wise (see, for example, Proverbs 3:1–8) do not sit well with the emphasis in Ecclesiastes on brevity and the lack of difference between the wise and the foolish (e.g., 2:14–15). A number of verses in Proverbs seem to be flatly contradicted in Ecclesiastes, such as when Proverbs contrasts the long lives of the pious with the short lives of the wicked (10:27), or promises that both righteous and wicked are repaid on earth (11:31). These differences have led some scholars even to detect in books like Job and Ecclesiastes a 'crisis' in wisdom literature, as if the Israelite sages who wrote Job and Ecclesiastes realised that life is not so well ordered and consistent as Proverbs seems to promise.[46] I think this is overstated, however. Although Proverbs and Ecclesiastes are strikingly different, Proverbs itself is clear that its promises do not always work out as quickly and neatly as a naïve reader might assume. For example, the book of Proverbs understands that sometimes the wicked are rich and the righteous are poor (15:16; 16:8–9; 19:1; 28:6); it also understands that sometimes those who fear the Lord suffer injustice or die before their time (1:11; 13:23; 24:11). There are other statements in Proverbs that

---

[46] See further James Crenshaw, *Old Testament Wisdom: An Introduction* (rev. ed.; Louisville: Westminster John Knox, 1998), 116–18; Leo Perdue, *Wisdom Literature: A Theological History* (Louisville: Westminster John Knox, 2007), 82–5, 185, 188–9.

almost sound as if they could come right out of Ecclesiastes (16:9; 21:30; 27:1).

All of this is to say that Proverbs does make extravagant promises to those willing to trust and fear God, but also gives wide room for those promises to come true slowly and in complicated ways – and perhaps not in this life at all.[47] This means, in turn, that there is less tension between Proverbs and Ecclesiastes than one might think, and we can see these books as giving different emphases instead of contradicting each other. On the one hand, Proverbs insists on the glorious future awaiting those who will trust God more than their own ideas about how life works (3:5–6). Ecclesiastes, without contradicting this (see 8:12–13), helps us to be sober and realistic about our expectations for life in a frustrated creation. That glorious future will come, but it may only very partially be realised in this life.

5. A strategy for reading Ecclesiastes

As we have seen above, even very attentive readers of the Bible can misapprehend the book of Ecclesiastes. How can we put ourselves in a position to hear everything God is saying to us in it? Three perspectives will be helpful to keep in mind.

First, the book is intentionally difficult to read, both in the sense of sometimes being difficult to understand and in the sense of being difficult to take. So if you wince in discomfort as you read, you're not doing anything wrong. It is not for nothing that Ecclesiastes 12:11 compares wisdom teachings to sheep goads which poke and provoke us to places we would not otherwise go. The proverb in 7:3 could stand as a motto for the whole:

---

[47] Bruce Waltke has a superb discussion of this aspect of Proverbs, including its eschatological dimension, in *The Book of Proverbs: Chapters 1–15* (Grand Rapids: Eerdmans, 2004), 104–9.

INTRODUCTION

'Vexation is better than laughter, for by an evil face the heart is made glad' (author's translation). There is a kind of vexation that leads to a deep joy but which takes from us easy, distracting pleasures ('laughter'). The Teacher Qohelet has a happier long-term goal, but he is trying to vex us. The frustration of the book is intentional.

But vexing us is not the only thing Qohelet wants to do. A second perspective to remember is that Qohelet's larger goal in vexing us is to make our heart glad – to help us rejoice, not just in eternity, but even in this earthly life.[48] In other words, Ecclesiastes in the context of the whole Bible wants to give us the best of both worlds: solid joy and hope in eternity, together with solid joy in our fading, earthly existence. What if we were able to enjoy life in such a way that 'the slings and arrows of outrageous fortune' could not take from us?[49] To rejoice in earthly life exactly as it is – without our enjoyment depending on our life always going well, or ignoring death, or how little we are actually in control of? That would be a very precious gift.

Third, let's remember the idea of 'bothness'. Ecclesiastes wants to show us that earthly life is both vanity and a gift, both frustrating and deeply good. In fact, part of what is so profound about the book is how it connects the two: we will never be able to receive life as good until we are properly and entirely frustrated with it.

This means we must resist the temptation to treat certain parts of the book as representing a position with which Qohelet disagrees, or thinking through a secular position to its hopeless end point. Rather, Qohelet wants us to despair of everything that will eventually let us down. We must be impoverished in

---

[48] Doug Ingram points out that Ecclesiastes uses the word 'good' fifty-two times in twelve chapters, more frequently than any other Old Testament book; *Ambiguity in Ecclesiastes* (London: T&T Clark, 2006), 169.

[49] William Shakespeare, *Hamlet*, act 3, scene 1.

this way if we are to follow Qohelet through to that full joy and true engagement with our fleeting, uncontrollable lives. It is difficult to inhabit both life's darkness and its joy, easier to default to one or the other (as the history of interpretation shows). As much as possible, let's stay in the awkward position of straddling both. It is deeply important for Christians to do so.

6. The shape of the book

The book of Ecclesiastes is not tightly organised, but some shape of the whole is evident. The main thesis and argument is given in 1:1–11. Then 1:12–2:26 are a past-tense narrative about how the Teacher came to the conclusions of 1:1–11. Qohelet finishes chapter 2 by recording his central insight into how best to engage with life under the sun; he then gives a happier restatement of his main argument in 3:1–15 from the perspectives of this new insight.

The main body of the book, in 3:16–10:20, is more loosely organised. In these chapters, Qohelet the Teacher works out his main thesis about vanity by observing something, reflecting and drawing conclusions, and moving on. There is something of a shift at 6:10–12, which summarises the book so far and functions as a transition. The phrase 'chasing of wind' occurs only in the first half of the book, and Qohelet will focus more on the unpredictability of the future in the second half. Otherwise, Qohelet just moves from one subject to another.

Chapters 11–12 have a kind of finality to them, providing a conclusion to the book. The section 11:1–6 is the most joyful Qohelet ever sounds, and the twofold command both to enjoy and to remember our approaching death in 11:7–12:8 is made in a climactic way. The book ends as the editor gives us the first commentary on Qohelet's words in 12:9–14.

Since chapters 3–10 are not ordered in any sequence I can

discern, I do not follow a numbered outline in this commentary. Here are the main sections:

> Introduction and main thesis: vanity of vanities (1:1–11)
> Qohelet's autobiography: three investigations (1:12–2:26)
>   Everything which is done (1:12–18)
>   The good life (2:1–11)
>   Wisdom (2:12–26)
> Everything beautiful in its time (3:1–15)
> Oppression (3:16–22)
> Five 'better-than' statements (4)
> True piety (5:1–7)
> Wealth and its enjoyment (5:8–6:9)
> What is really good? (6:10–7:14)
> Righteousness and wisdom subject to vanity (7:15–29)
> Acting wisely before the king (8:1–9)
> The problem of delayed judgment (8:10–17)
> Death as a catalyst to joy (9)
> Various proverbs (10)
> Generous work (11:1–6) before a cosmic funeral (11:7–12:8)
> Editor's conclusion (12:9–14)

Preachers looking for guidance on how to divide the book up for a sermon series are encouraged to begin with 1:1–11 as an opening to the book. (There may need to be encouragements to your congregation that not all of the book will be this gloomy!) It is then helpful to focus on 1:12–2:26 and consider how Qohelet reached the conclusions of 1:1–11. The insight that life is a gift, which ends chapter 2, can act as an inducement to come back next week, with your third sermon focusing on Qohelet's great insight in 3:1–15 that life has value as a gift from God, not as an opportunity for us to establish our significance through work. With regard to 3:16–10:20, I am not convinced it is necessary to preach every verse; perhaps church small groups could focus on the passages that are not preached on. I personally find 3:16–22; 4:17–5:6; 6:10–7:14; 7:15–29 and chapter 9 especially significant and helpful. The series could appropriately close with Qohelet's own conclusion in 11:1–12:8, perhaps also with some reflections on how the final verses of the book (12:9–14) guide us in reading it.

1

Introduction and Main Thesis: Vanity of Vanities!

ECCLESIASTES 1:1–11

Behind our work is a desire for permanent achievement and significance in this life (verse 3). Because the accomplishments of our life's work are soon erased, however, our lives fail to achieve this purpose, and so are in vain (verse 2). The natural order witnesses to this (verses 4–7). Humanity is stuck in the same patterns (verses 9–11), unable to produce anything new or lasting.

Everything is meaningless

1 The words of the Teacher,[a] son of David, king of Jerusalem:

2 'Meaningless! Meaningless!'
  says the Teacher.
  'Utterly meaningless!
  Everything is meaningless.'
3 What do people gain from all
    their labours
  at which they toil under the
    sun?
4 Generations come and generations go,
  but the earth remains for
    ever.
5 The sun rises and the sun sets,
  and hurries back to where it
    rises.
6 The wind blows to the south
  and turns to the north;
  round and round it goes,
  ever returning on its course.
7 All streams flow into the sea,
  yet the sea is never full.
  To the place the streams come
    from,
  there they return again.
8 All things are wearisome,
  more than one can say.
  The eye never has enough of
    seeing,

> nor the ear its fill of hearing.
> ⁹ What has been will be again,
>   what has been done will be done again;
>   there is nothing new under the sun.
> ¹⁰ Is there anything of which one can say,
>   'Look! This is something new'?
>   It was here already, long ago;
>   it was here before our time.
> ¹¹ No one remembers the former generations,
>   and even those yet to come
>   will not be remembered
>   by those who follow them.

---

a 1 Or *the leader of the assembly*; also in verses 2 and 12

1. Title • *Ecclesiastes 1:1*

The book begins by telling us its main speaker (the Teacher), his pedigree and ancestry (son of David) and his role (king). This information both locates and authenticates the wisdom of the book. Since kings were (ideally) profound in their wisdom (see Proverbs 1:1 and 25:1, as well as 16:10; 20:8; 25:2–3), Ecclesiastes is not just anonymous good advice. Royal authority and insight stand behind it.

Attentive readers will quickly learn, however, that two voices speak in the book: the Teacher and an anonymous writer. We know this because someone speaks about Qohelet in the third person in 7:27 and 12:8, even evaluating the Teacher for us in 12:9–14. While authors can, of course, refer to themselves in the third person, it would be strange for them to do so in the middle of a first-person sentence (see 7:27). It would also be strange for an author to recommend his own work within his own text – imagine the present author including in this commentary the sentence, 'Ortlund worked very hard on this book and was insightful about Ecclesiastes' (compare 12:9–10). Aside from the presence of this second author, however, we can say nothing about him; he gives us no clues whatsoever as to his identity. All he does is pass on the Teacher's words with a warm recommendation.

INTRODUCTION AND MAIN THESIS

As for the first voice in the book, many have identified the Teacher with King Solomon. This identification is natural, for there was only one son of David (1:1) who reigned over all Israel (verse 12; 1 Kings 12 records how the kingdom split under the foolish reign of Solomon's son Rehoboam). The fact that Solomon was renowned for his wisdom makes it even easier to imagine him penning this comprehensive investigation into what is good for humans in whatever time they have (see 2:3).

There is another way to interpret these Solomonic hints in Ecclesiastes, however, which I think better accords with the book's original purpose. I do not want to make too much of whether or not Solomon wrote Ecclesiastes, for any Christian can receive this book as God's word regardless of who they believe wrote it. I am very happy for readers to draw their own conclusions.[1] But the reader should be aware of the strong hints that the second anonymous author gives that the Teacher is a literary creation, a persona, with a calculated rhetorical purpose.

Perhaps the strongest hint is that Solomon is never directly named. (Well-intentioned readers who insist on Solomonic authorship go beyond the evidence of the text.) The word standing behind the NIV's 'Teacher' (in Hebrew, *qōhelet*) is not a proper name, but a job title: a leader or teacher in the religious assembly (see 12:9).[2] This is confirmed in 12:8, where we read of 'the Qohelet' (the definite article is not added to proper

---

[1] J. I. Packer, who loved Ecclesiastes, categorically states that it does not matter whether or not Solomon wrote the book. See Packer, *Knowing God* (London: Hodder and Stoughton, 1973), 93. Packer gives a short but penetrating discussion of Ecclesiastes in *Knowing God*, 93–7.

[2] Biblical Hebrew can use a feminine singular noun derived from a verb to denote male occupations, such as the word for 'scribe' (*sōpheret*, from *sāphar*, 'to write' (Ezra 2:55; Nehemiah 7:57)). The verb related to *qōhelet* is *qāhal*, 'to assemble', repeatedly used for the religious assembly in the Pentateuch (e.g., Leviticus 4:13; Numbers 1:18). It is also used in 1 Kings 8:1 to describe Solomon assembling all Israel for the dedication of the Temple.

names in biblical Hebrew). 'The Qohelet' might, of course, be a way of referring to Solomon, but Solomon is named directly as the author in other parts of the Old Testament (see Proverbs 1:1; 25:1; Song of Songs 1:1; Psalms 72:1; 127:1). What is gained by describing one of Israel's most famous kings indirectly?[3] No one would pass up a chance to read a reflection on life from Israel's wisest king. If Solomon were the author, I cannot think of any reason not to say so. It would also be strange for a second anonymous voice to feel the need to recommend a book by Solomon, of all people, to later readers (12:9–14).

Another related factor against Solomonic authorship is the Hebrew of Ecclesiastes, which does not appear to be pre-exilic. All languages change over time, and biblical languages are no exception. In the particular case of Ecclesiastes, there are characteristic markers that put it in the post-exilic period, centuries after Solomon. Of course, reconstructing the historical development of an ancient language is a tricky business, and perhaps access to more ancient Hebrew manuscripts would change the current picture of how Hebrew changed over time.[4] Without ignoring these cautions, however, readers should be aware that what evidence exists points to Ecclesiastes being closer linguistically to books like Esther or 1 and 2 Chronicles than books

---

[3] Readers who insist on 'Teacher' as a code name for Solomon can run into other difficulties. The great Jewish exegete Rashi, for example, argued that Qohelet is a code name for Solomon because Solomon 'assembled' many proverbs – and then went on to argue that Proverbs 30 was written by Solomon as well, even though the author Agur is listed in verse 1. Rashi does this by appealing to the Hebrew verb *'āgar*, which means 'to gather' (as in Proverbs 6:8) – so Solomon is the 'gatherer'; see *Miqra'ot Gedolot HaKeter: Hamesh Megillot*, 124. But this is implausible; Agur is a perfectly good Hebrew name. If we follow this line of argument, how many other biblical authors will turn out to be Solomon in disguise?

[4] See the appropriate cautions registered by Ian Young, 'Is the Prose Tale of Job in Late Biblical Hebrew?', *Vetus Testamentum* 59 (2009): 606–29.

written before the exile. There are individual words and other markers that make it 'sound' as if someone living centuries after Solomon had written this book.[5]

In light of all this, my sense is that we should not take the Solomonic hints in Ecclesiastes 1–2 as evidence that Solomon wrote Ecclesiastes. In leaving Qohelet the Teacher unnamed, the text is hinting that Qohelet is not a real historical person, but a literary persona with Solomon-like wisdom. His purpose in creating this literary character is to help us accept shocking claims we might otherwise be tempted to dismiss. It is a way of saying, 'Imagine a person as intelligent and skilled as Solomon and with the unlimited resources of a king: no one will ever tell him that there's no room in the budget for some plan of his. He has both the means and the know-how to do anything he sets his mind to. If anyone could be happy with life under the sun, it would be him, right? But he was actually one of the most depressed people ever. Let's see why.'

In interpreting the word *qōhelet* this way, I am certainly not claiming that the Scriptures are trying to deceive us. The author makes it clear that he is not presenting Qohelet as an actual historical person by leaving him unnamed.

There is a second reason why we need not see any deception here, which is a little more involved. It has to do with a particular literary convention from the ancient Middle East which Ecclesiastes evokes in its portrayal of Qohelet.

There are multiple examples from the biblical world of

---

[5] Among a number of other examples, two Persian loanwords are found in Ecclesiastes: *pardēs*, 'park' (2:5, literally 'paradise') and *pitgām*, 'sentence, decree' (8:11). Neither is attested before the fifth century BC. Examples of other indications of a later date include the shorter form of the first person independent personal pronoun, the more frequent use of the shorter form of the relative pronoun, more frequent Aramaic terms and the relative absence of the consecutive imperfect. See further the essays in the fourth section of Boda, Longman and Rata (eds.), *The Words of the Wise Are like Goads*, 283–363.

narratives about kings, written by scribes in the first person, as if the king himself were speaking.[6] Some were even written posthumously.[7] These texts wax eloquent about the king's lifetime of achievements, especially their building projects (compare Ecclesiastes 2:4–8); they often show the king comparing himself favourably with his predecessors (see 2:9). It was understood that the king need not himself have been the direct author of every word, even when these texts read, 'I, King So-and-So, did such and such.' Deception was not the goal, but celebrating and memorialising the king's reign.

The similarities between these texts and Ecclesiastes suggests that Ecclesiastes intends to evoke this literary convention. We are given the words of a man with royal privilege and resources who reflects on his lifetime of achievements, but who is never given a real name, known only as 'Qohelet', the Teacher. No claim to an actual king is intended; the author is activating the network of associations surrounding this genre in the biblical world and twisting them for his own purposes. The 'twist' comes in the way that other texts in this genre are not nearly as bleak as Ecclesiastes; every other king found it easy to enjoy his accomplishments. In this book, however, we read about one more king, but instead of finding satisfaction, we hear the bitter wisdom he

---

[6] Some examples of this would include the Mesha inscription, the Zakkur inscription and the Cyrus Cylinder. Those interested can read these texts in William Hallo and K. Lawson Younger, Jr (eds.), *The Context of Scripture, Volume 2: Monumental Inscriptions from the Biblical World* (Leiden: Brill, 2003), 137–8, 155, 315–16, respectively. More discussion is given in Martin Shields, 'Qohelet and Royal Autobiography', in Boda, Longman and Rata (eds.), *The Words of the Wise are Like Goads*, 117–136; Seow, *Ecclesiastes*, 98–99, 119, 144–5; Fox, *A Time to Tear Down*, 153–5.

[7] Such as the Legend of Sargon, written in the seventh century BC about a king living around 2300 BC; see William Hallo and K. Lawson Younger, Jr (eds.), *The Context of Scripture, Volume 1: Canonical Compositions from the Biblical World* (Leiden: Brill, 2003), 416.

gained about vanity and true contentment 'under the sun'. This strategy prevents at the outset the reader rejecting the difficult truths in this book by thinking, 'If I had more money and time and resources – if I could just bring that particular pipe dream into reality – then I could finally be really happy.' The Teacher had everything, and he came to hate life (2:17) – for a time. This imaginative space creates a context where we can consider more deeply truths that are easy to avoid.

2. Main thesis: vanity • *Ecclesiastes 1:2*

The book's second verse is Qohelet's main teaching and the single major piece of wisdom he wants to pass on. Although Qohelet will grow and change over the course of the book, he never surrenders this interpretation of the human condition after the fall: he ends his teaching identically to how he began (see 12:8) and persistently returns to it in each chapter (the word translated as 'meaningless' by the NIV is repeated thirty-seven times). Qohelet will not let us get away from this. This means that we must take our time with verse 2 if we are to understand anything in the book at all.

The NIV translates the Hebrew word beginning verse 2 (*hebel*) as, 'Meaningless! Meaningless!' While I regard the NIV as a good translation and a trustworthy guide to God's word, its rendering of this word is indefensible, and (doubtless unintentionally) puts the reader at a great disadvantage in trying to understand this difficult book. There are multiple reasons why. To begin with, Qohelet says in 11:9–10 that youth should be enjoyed because it is *hebel*. But if youth is 'meaningless', how can that count as a reason to enjoy it? On the other hand, if *hebel* means something like 'fleeting', the verse makes perfect sense: enjoy youth before it is gone. Qohelet will also describe situations or events as *hebel* when they plainly are not meaningless – the meaning they have might be very unfortunate, but they have a meaning. For example, a stranger enjoying another's labour (2:19; 6:2) or the delays in God's judgment of wickedness (7:15; 8:14) are described by Qohelet as *hebel*. But it makes no sense to say that God (apparently) allowing evil to flourish is meaningless. This troubling situation (who has not witnessed it?) has a meaning, one contrary to all reasonable expectation. God should confront, expose, condemn and stop evil; but frequently it seems to run wild. This is not meaningless; the meaning appears to be that God is not doing what he should.

Other intractable problems dog the NIV's translation of this word. If everything is meaningless, why would Qohelet recommend some things as better than others (e.g., 3:12; 4:6; 5:5)?[8] Surely total meaninglessness renders such comparisons empty? Why bother saying that wisdom is unqualifiedly better than folly (2:13) and that we should fear God (3:14; 5:7)? Furthermore, if everything is meaningless, why does God bring everything under his judgment, whether good or evil (12:14)? Why would God even care, if nothing has any significance?

Even more damaging for this translation is Qohelet's identification of everything in life as a gift from God (2:24–6; 5:17–18; 8:15; 9:9). Are God's gifts meaningless? Surely the identity of the Giver makes them richly meaningful? To translate 1:2 as 'Meaningless!' makes the book contradictory. While I appreciate the way the NIV gives modern Western readers an opportunity to connect with the book, the idea of meaninglessness is foreign to Ecclesiastes, and (I would argue) to the Old Testament as a whole. It is not so much the question of meaning that exercises Qohelet as value: what is good for human beings to do, during whatever time they have (see 2:3).[9]

---

[8] Jason DeRouchie, 'Shepherding Wind and One Wise Shepherd: Grasping for Breath in Ecclesiastes', *Southern Baptist Journal of Theology* 15 (2011): 7.

[9] See further Derek Kidner, *Wisdom to Live By: An Introduction to the Old*

If 'meaningless' will not do, how should we render Qohelet's favourite word in English? The first thing to do is to get clear on what the word means outside the book of Ecclesiastes. The word *hebel* is used in three main ways elsewhere in the Old Testament. First, it means 'breath', or, by extension, something fleeting and impermanent. Isaiah thus speaks of a 'breath' carrying off idols (57:13), and elsewhere Job asks to be left alone, because he will not live forever, but his days are *hebel*, gone quickly (7:16).[10]

Second, the word can mean something that is in vain, pointless, empty or deceitful. The Suffering Servant of Isaiah uses this word to describe the apparent failure of his ministry in Isaiah 49:4. Earlier in his book, Isaiah uses the word to describe Egypt's useless military help (30:7). Job uses it as well to question what the point of arguing with God is, since he thinks he will be condemned regardless of what he says (9:29).[11] Finally, the word can refer to idols.[12]

Since Ecclesiastes never discusses idolatry, we can leave this

---

Testament's Wisdom Books (Leicester: IVP, 1985), 100–4. Of course, one of the senses of the word 'meaningless' is 'pointless' (at least in common usage), and I will argue below that an important aspect of Qohelet's use of *hebel* is futility or vanity, just in this sense. But another sense of 'meaningless' can be something without any semantic content or truth – something incoherent, incomprehensible, with nothing there to understand. Qohelet definitely does not think life is 'meaningless' in this sense, and since there are other ways in English to communicate pointlessness, the NIV's choice introduces more confusion than clarity.

[10] The NIV translates as 'have no meaning' here, but I think wrongly; within the verse, Job is speaking about his soon-approaching death, not a lack of meaning. For other Old Testament uses of *hebel* with this sense, see Psalms 39:5; 62:9 (something weightless); 78:33; 144:4; Proverbs 13:11; 21:6.

[11] Other Old Testament uses of this word with this sense can be found in Job 27:12; 35:16; Psalms 39:7; 94:11; Jeremiah 10:3, 15; 23:16; Lamentations 4:17. It is parallel to 'falsehood' in Job 21:34; Proverbs 31:30 and Zechariah 10:2.

[12] Deuteronomy 32:12; 1 Kings 16:13, 26; 2 Kings 17:15; Psalms 31:6; 62:10; Jeremiah 8:19; 10:8; 14:22; Jonah 2:8.

final use of *hebel* out of the discussion; but otherwise, let us note that *hebel* has a well-defined sense of 'breath' or something gone quickly, or (by extension) something in vain, failing to achieve its goal, futile or pointless. As we turn to Qohelet's use of *hebel*, we will see that it fits these patterns and also moves beyond them.

Before looking at *hebel* in Ecclesiastes, however, please notice that several occurrences of the word outside Ecclesiastes show it being used in different senses within the same passage, such as Psalm 39:5–6, which moves from 'fleeting' (verse 5, my translation) to 'in vain' (verse 6), or Jeremiah 2:5, which uses the word to refer to idols, and then the emptying effect this had on Israel. There is a certain fluidity to the term which makes it difficult to find a single English equivalent. We will see the same in Qohelet's use of the word.

Turning to Ecclesiastes, we see that Qohelet will sometimes speak of *hebel* as something fleeting, but more frequently his use of the word conforms to the second definition given above: something in vain or not achieving its purpose. With regard to the former, 11:10 is a good example: since *hebel* is stated as the reason to enjoy being young, it must mean 'fleeting' here, since nothing else would count as a motivation to enjoy youth.

Qohelet will more frequently speak of things or situations as *hebel* in the sense of their being 'in vain', failing to achieve their goal or satisfy our expectations for them. His frequent pairing of *hebel* with 'chasing after the wind' (1:14; 2:11, 17, 26; 4:4, 16; 6:9) strongly recommends 'in vain' as a translation here. What is more futile or pointless than that?

The same nuance resurfaces elsewhere in the book. In 2:1–2, he says pleasure is *hebel* and then asks, 'What does pleasure accomplish?' The implied answer – nothing, or, at least, nothing that lasts – makes 'vanity' a good translation. Similarly, in 2:15–17, Qohelet realises that the wise will die like the fool, and then asks why he has bothered to be so wise. It seems that he wanted something from wisdom which it did not give him – so wisdom is (in some sense) 'in vain'.

Another example is found in 6:11. Human beings cannot contend with how God has set up reality, and talking or arguing or planning a lot will not change that. Such words do not profit anyone and are thus 'in vain'.

This means that Qohelet is using the word *hebel* in expected ways, and that we are already a good way towards understanding what he wants to teach us: our lives are over very quickly, and we tend to expect something from life under the sun which it does not and cannot give us. As a result, a pointlessness or futility pervades our already-short lives.

But some of Qohelet's uses of *hebel* do not fit the meaning of 'fleeting' or 'in vain'. For example, Qohelet more than once complains about leaving our life's labours to a stranger (2:19–23; 4:7–8). Especially in chapter 2, this vexes him deeply: not only will Qohelet no longer be able to enjoy all he worked for so tirelessly, but he also has absolutely no control over whether all his work will be stewarded well or squandered. Qohelet then says this situation is *hebel*. 'Fleeting' or 'ephemeral' will not do as a translation, because the point is exactly that Qohelet's work will live on after him – his life might be fleeting, but his life's work is not. 'Pointless' or 'futile' might work in the sense that Qohelet worked really hard in order to enjoy it (see comments below on chapter 2); but it is not so much Qohelet's perception of his own work that is under examination in this passage, but the fact that someone else will enjoy what Qohelet laboured for. The disproportion between effort and result, the incongruity, is what Qohelet says is *hebel*.

There are multiple other examples in Ecclesiastes where Qohelet describes something as *hebel* in the sense of a disproportion, a ridiculous incongruity, something contrary and offensive to all reasonable expectation. This is the case when a successful new ruler rises from inauspicious circumstances to great fame and power, only to be forgotten in the end (4:16); when people sin brazenly and enjoy great lives, while the best of lives are sometimes cut unexpectedly short (7:15; 8:14); and also when the wicked are praised after their death (8:10). A sense of, 'It just shouldn't be this way!' pervades these passages. None of these situations is fleeting (they sometimes last a long time), and it does not seem quite right to call them pointless or without purpose. 'Absurd' seems to be the best way to capture the idea in these cases, in the sense of 'contrary to reasonable expectation'.[13] As far as I am aware, this is innovative; the word *hebel* is not used in this way outside Ecclesiastes. (As we will see below, this is not the only way in which Qohelet manipulates Hebrew in unique ways.)

We can account for all of Qohelet's uses of *hebel* according to these three meanings: brief or fleeting, pointless or futile, and absurd. In some cases, one of these meanings is clearly in view (such as 11:10). Often, however, it can be difficult to decide. More than once Qohelet implies that the brevity of our lives makes them pointless (we are working for some kind of permanence which we never get), leading to an absurd incongruity between effort and result.

This makes it difficult to translate Qohelet's use of *hebel* with a single English word. In this commentary, I will use 'vanity' or 'in vain' in place of the NIV's 'meaningless'.[14] I know the term is not commonly used today, but it seems the least-worst option to communicate the varied nuances with which Qohelet uses it. Nevertheless, I hope readers remember the simultaneous hints of brevity, futility and absurdity when I speak of 'vanity' in Ecclesiastes. Jacques Ellul makes a similar point when he writes that *hebel* implies, 'as for its reality, it is insubstantial; from point

---

[13] This is Michael Fox's translation in *A Time to Tear Down*. Fox, however, translates every example of *hebel* this way, which is unconvincing (again, with regard to 11:9–10, absurdity is not the reason why youth should be enjoyed). But it does seem valid in some instances.
[14] Many other translations have been suggested, including 'breath', 'enigma', 'senselessness/nonsense'. See Fox, *A Time to Tear Down*, 27–42, for a longer list.

of view of the truth, a lie; with regard to efficiency, useless; with regard to security, deceitful'.[15]

This is the essence of Qohelet's wisdom. Qohelet will unfold for us throughout the book all that this means, how he came to this conclusion and how we should live in light of it; but he does not wait or hesitate to confront us immediately with the reality of the brevity, futility and absurdity of life after the fall. Every word in verse 2 is calculated to make us feel the pervasive weight of *hebel*: the first phrase in Hebrew is *hăbēl hăbālîm*, 'hebel of hebels', 'vanity of vanities!' The superlative genitive, like 'Lord of lords' or 'Song of songs', means there is no limit to the futility to which our lives are subject. As if that were not enough, he repeats this in the second clause, and then adds 'all' is *hebel* – that is, *hebel* touches and pervades every aspect of life under the sun. There is no area we can section off and quarantine from it; it contaminates everything. In fact, *hebel* contaminates the whole of the verse itself: *hebel* is the first and last word, and occurs five times in the eight Hebrew words of the line. The final phrase in Hebrew (*hakōl hābel*) is also slightly shorter than the first two (*habēl hăbālîm*), creating a note of finality: *hăbēl hăbālîm – hăbēl hăbālîm – hakōl hābel*. There is no room for escape.

It is helpful to remember that Ecclesiastes is wisdom literature, to be read along with books like Proverbs and Job. Old Testament wisdom can be defined as 'competence with regard to the complexities of creation'.[16] This means that wisdom is not just being smart; indeed, highly intelligent and skilled people can count as 'fools' according to this part of Scripture. Rather, just as there is a physical and natural orderliness in God's world, the

---

[15] Jacques Ellul, *Reason for Being: A Meditation on Ecclesiastes*, trans. Joyce Hanks (Grand Rapids: Eerdmans, 1990), 52.

[16] This lovely phrase is Tim Keller's; he used it repeatedly in his preaching on Old Testament wisdom books. See further Tim Keller's podcast, 'Training in Wisdom', recorded on 3 November 2021, www.oneplace.com/ministries/gospel-in-life/listen/training-in-wisdom-928470.html (accessed 22 September 2023).

Old Testament teaches that there is a moral and spiritual orderliness as well (Proverbs 3:19–20). This moral order is, however, not obvious or easy to discern, but complex. As a result, young Israelites entering into adult responsibility need teaching from elders that ultimately comes from God (see Proverbs 2:6) about how to live well and successfully within the non-obvious patterns of God's moral order. It is not obvious to most teenagers, for example, that a soft word turns away anger (Proverbs 15:1), or that sin eventually destroys itself (Proverbs 14:32) or that ceaseless chattering can be deeply dangerous spiritually (Proverbs 13:3). But those who receive and obey this counter-intuitive wisdom have the richest of blessings awaiting them (Proverbs 3:1–12).

Ecclesiastes aligns itself with this tradition of wise insight into the complexities of creation in multiple ways, and not least when the author addresses the reader as 'my son' (12:12). This echoes the many references to fathers teaching sons in Proverbs (Proverbs 1:8, 10, 15; 2:1; 3:1 and so on).[17] But Ecclesiastes does not merely repeat Proverbs. Where Proverbs is more wide-ranging, Qohelet teaches us about one aspect in particular of God's ordering of human life and how to live wisely within it: God's subjection of all things to frustration (Romans 8:19–20). 'Frustration' would not work as a translation of *hebel*, but the idea seems close to *hebel* in Ecclesiastes. We can never quite get our lives entirely under our control and working the way we want – and then it all slips through our fingers and we go to the grave.

So how best to live? Ecclesiastes is the one book in the canon specifically designed to help engage with ordinary life after the fall and before the eschaton.

---

[17] The references to 'my son' do not mean that wisdom was only taught to young men; mothers were equally involved in this teaching, having been taught when they were young (see Proverbs 1:8; 6:8; 23:22; 31:1). It is rather an invitation for all readers of Proverbs, whether male or female or young or old, to imagine themselves again as a teenager just entering into adult responsibility and learning about the complications of adult life and relationships.

INTRODUCTION AND MAIN THESIS

Qohelet's wisdom about enjoying a creation subjected to frustration will be useless to us, however, unless we closely attend to and receive the difficult and troubling things he has to teach us. Qohelet certainly does not ease us into his teaching gently. Even the summary of his teaching in 1:2 can be overwhelming. It is difficult to be faced so squarely with how quickly our lives fade, how little we accomplish, and the distortions and absurdities we cannot iron out. I ask every reader, however, to expose themselves to everything Ecclesiastes has to say to us. The book itself tells us it is given to us by God (12:11). And there simply is no other way to reach the unstinting joy that Qohelet has in this life (9:7–9).

Please be aware that when Qohelet says, 'All is *hebel*,' he is most emphatically not saying that everything is bad. Indeed, his book is the one place in all of Scripture that gives an enthusiastic and unambiguous command to enjoy life in the here and now. The fact that God – for wise reasons that will become clearer as we read – has imposed on creation limitation and frustration does not mean that life 'under the sun' is bad, any more than God's curses on the serpent, Eve and Adam (Genesis 3:14–19) destroy the goodness of his world. God does limit and (to an extent) frustrate the abundance and fecundity and vitality of his world as life is eked out by sweat and dust returns to dust. But creation is still good and very good (1 Timothy 4:4–5) and should be received as such. In fact, Qohelet's counter-intuitive wisdom will teach us that the only way truly to bask in that goodness is by resolutely facing up to the frustration of our lives under God's hand.

Furthermore, it is important to remember that Qohelet is not a cynic. He will never even so much as hint that obeying God does not matter, or that wisdom is not worth having, or that the absurdities of life mean that we should never expect anything from God. Christian discipleship and spirituality – Qohelet's term for this is to fear the Lord (3:14; 5:7; 7:18; 8:12–13) – are unambiguously commended by the book, and folly and disobedience condemned. Qohelet urges us to remember, however, that even these good and necessary things are subject to *hebel*. We will not always receive from them the benefits we can reasonably expect. We will return to this in later chapters, but it is important to state it now, because Qohelet's teaching can be so discouraging that it can be tempting to try to isolate being a Christian from the futility and vanity of life: in this area of my being (we might tell ourselves), frustration and disappointment will never reach me. I think we see this temptation in how people have read Ecclesiastes in earlier centuries (see Introduction). But Qohelet will not allow this. All is *hebel*, he says, even good things, even those things God commands us. The reader who can receive this will find a joy which even life's craziest twists cannot shake (see further 7:15–18).

3. Basic question: what gain is there? • Ecclesiastes 1:3

Verse 2 is Qohelet's basic thesis about life under the sun. Verse 3 is the prior question he asked of life which led him to the conclusion of verse 2. The NIV's 'gain' is a good translation of *yitrôn*, a word that Qohelet will repeat and which is an important part of his wisdom (see 2:11, 13; 3:9; 5:8, 15; 7:12; 10:10–11).[18] It is derived from a verb which means 'to be left over' (such as referring to the trees and plants left over from the plague of hail in Exodus 10:15). Qohelet will use it in two ways.

First, Qohelet will speak of *yitrôn* as 'gain' in the sense of 'advantage' – something better than something else which benefits the owner (see 2:13; 5:8; 7:12; 10:10–11). But Qohelet

---

[18] Although the verb and related nouns recur in the Old Testament, this particular noun is found only in Ecclesiastes, and seems to be one more example of the author using Hebrew in new ways to express his wisdom.

INTRODUCTION AND MAIN THESIS

will also speak of *yitrôn* as an expected gain or profit from work (see also 2:11; 3:9; 5:15). The 'left over' gain in focus in these verses is not just a paycheque or a company you built or a computer program you designed. It denotes what is left over from a lifetime of labour, the total result of 'all their labours at which they toil'.

In 1:3, Qohelet asks what gain there is from a lifetime of labour in this second sense. He is asking about the total effect of our lives. A note of weariness is sounded: he repeats the word for 'labour' twice (*'āmal*, translated as 'labours' and 'toil'), and the form of the verb could be translated as 'the work at which they keep on labouring'.[19] Qohelet does not answer the question he asks, but the answer is obvious, and impresses itself on us more powerfully for remaining unspoken. What remains, what is left over, from the days and decades spent at work? Irrespective of little gains and losses along the way, what permanent gain do we get? All those paycheques cashed – but what lasting profit can we hold on to from all those long years of labour? The answer: nothing. Whatever we gain or lose on the way, the total effect of our lives is zero. We are drawing lines in the sand and the tide is coming in. Looking at our lives from a wide-angle lens, we accomplish nothing permanent and have nothing to show for all the years we spend working. As a result, our lives are *hebel* (verse 2). We quickly fade away, and our labour is pointless, because we get nothing from it in the end. How strange, how incongruous, that so much effort and stress and worry is spent, all to have it slip through our fingers.

Another depressing verse from Qohelet! We are only three verses into the book and already we smart under the sting of the words of the wise (12:11). Perhaps the reader is ready to close

---

[19] The imperfect verb is a progressive present (WOC 31.3b). The noun form derived from the verb sometimes has the sense of trouble or wearying toil (e.g., Genesis 41:51; Deuteronomy 26:7; Psalm 90:10).

the book and read something else, or is worried that Qohelet is being unbiblical. What about our reward when we stand before Christ at the end of the age (Matthew 25:21)? Surely, if anything counts as permanent gain, it is that. And doesn't Paul specifically say that our labour in the Lord is not in vain (1 Corinthians 15:58)?

The last phrase of the verse is helpful as we reflect on these questions: 'under the sun'. Qohelet signals to us here that he is limiting the sphere of his inquiry to this earthly life (it recurs twenty-seven times in the book). The phrase is spatial – on earth, not in heaven – but is also temporal. We know this because, although the phrase is not found elsewhere in the Old Testament, it is found in two inscriptions on tombs in Phoenicia, 'under the sun' standing in contrast to 'resting among the shades' in the grave.[20] This means that 'under the sun' can be a way of referring to the time of our earthly lives.

Now, it is important to emphasise that Qohelet did believe in a reality 'above the sun' (see 3:11; 12:7). However, he says almost nothing about it, because to do so might make it easier for readers to look away from the hard truths about brevity and vanity that he wants us to face. Ecclesiastes is the Bible's one book that rigorously focuses on living wisely in this age, before the eschaton. This focus means that we should not set his teaching against the New Testament's wonderful promises of eschatological reward in the age to come. When Paul says our labour in the Lord is not in vain (1 Corinthians 15:58), there is no contradiction with Ecclesiastes, for Paul is speaking of the new creation. Indeed, Ecclesiastes affirms this final reward (12:14).

But we are not yet at the comforting promise of the final verse of Ecclesiastes, or even close. We must allow Qohelet to confront us with truths we know but find convenient to avoid. He is trying to pry from us (not ungently) all the usual

---

[20] See Seow, *Ecclesiastes*, 105, for the texts and translations.

reasons we have for getting out of bed and slogging through another Tuesday morning, because most of the reasons we give ourselves are actually illusions. Would the reader agree with me when I say that I find a deep tendency to tell myself that my work matters because of the difference I am making? That the reason it is worth continuing in all my labour at which I toil is that the different communities I'm a part of are better for me having been there? All so that, when it comes time to retire, we can be satisfied with our total contribution (= 'gain' of verse 3)? Do you find that you make a similar link between the worth of your work and whatever visible results it has?

Qohelet certainly does not deny good gains along the way from our work or forbid us from enjoying them (compare 2:10 with 2:11; see also 11:1–6). But there is something inside that wants more than local, occasional gains. We hanker after something permanent, and we tend to link the value of our work with the long-term difference we make. I do, at least, and I suspect I am not the only one. But the Bible itself tells us that we do not make any long-term difference under the sun. This is hard to face up to. But we must allow Qohelet to push us into a place where we feel like giving up, where life and work really feel completely pointless (all so that he can give us a far more joyful reason for embracing our *hebel* existence). After all, Qohelet is right. However much we accomplish in this life, it is a matter of time until the mark we make is wiped away, we will be utterly forgotten, and it will be as if we never existed.

David Gibson puts it this way:

> You gain nothing from grinding your fingers to the bone, because the world will go on impervious to what you've done, and it will not remember you anyway . . . Ecclesiastes is a meditation on how life seems to elude our grasp in terms of lasting significance. If we try to gain control of the

world and our lives by what we can understand and by what we can do, we find that the control we seek eludes us.[21]

Receiving everything God's word has to say to us, and receiving the wisdom of this particular book, means deeply accepting this uncomfortable truth.

4. Evidence for vanity from the created order • *Ecclesiastes 1:4–7*

Qohelet does not merely assert the vanity of life under the sun; he argues for it, providing evidence from creation.[22] The descriptions of human generations, the sun, the wind and the rivers in these verses give an almost dizzying sense of business which is entirely useless, because nothing changes.[23] Generations come and go, come and go; the earth we walk on stands unchanged (verse 4). The sun rises and sets, rises and sets, hurrying (literally 'panting') to go right back to the same place and do it all over again (verse 5). The wind whips around, only to return on its course and whip around again (verse 6).[24] Rivers never stop flowing, but there is no fullness or finality when they empty into the sea; their water returns as rain and they keep on flowing (verse 7). Poetry in the Old Testament normally evokes a sense

---

[21] Gibson, *Destiny*, 12, 5.

[22] This is a common tactic in Old Testament wisdom literature (see, among other examples, Proverbs 6:6–11; Job 8:11–19; 12:7–9; 14:7–12). The underlying idea is that the natural order of God's world reflects its moral and spiritual order, such that one can be inferred from the other.

[23] The participles in these verses show repeated or continuous action (WOC 37.6d): 'keeps on going, keeps on turning', etc.

[24] Qohelet actually delays the noun 'the wind' to the end of the sentence: 'Going north, turning south, turning, turning, goes the wind; and on its course the wind returns.' It heightens the sense of frantic but empty repetition.

of heightening or intensification from one clause to the next and one line to the next, but there is no forward movement here, only a sense of aimless wandering, repetition without gain.[25]

If we want to know if Ecclesiastes 1:2–3 is true, all we have to do is open our eyes. Nature itself shows repetition without progress (verses 5–7) which makes no permanent change ('the earth remains forever', verse 4).[26] Generation after generation has trudged to work, raised families, fought and talked and feasted and died; the earth still stands. If they cannot produce any lasting or permanent change in the world – much less the sun and wind, which have been at their business for millennia uncounted – what makes us think we will? There is no gain for all our *hebel*-labour. Our lives don't really go anywhere. There is no hope for progress in these verses, no satisfaction of our desire for something permanently lasting which would endure through these repeating patterns.[27] Qohelet only points to human limitation.

5. Reaction: weariness • Ecclesiastes 1:8

Paradoxically, statements about the weary, endless repetitions of the world are themselves wearying. Stating the vanity of the world is itself tiring. There is no relief or refuge in diagnosing the nature of life under the sun, even when we do it accurately. Qohelet will not allow us any hope of escaping to some neutral vantage point by which articulating the world's vanity might

---

[25] As Tewoldemedhin Habtu writes, 'There is constant movement, but none of it is getting anywhere.' See 'Ecclesiastes', in *Africa Bible Commentary*, ed. Tokunboh Adeyemo (Grand Rapids: Zondervan, 2006), 788.

[26] Stuart Weeks, *A Critical and Exegetical Commentary on Ecclesiastes, Volume 1: Introduction and Commentary on Ecclesiastes 1.1–5.6* (London: T&T Clark, 2020), 262–3; Caneday, 'Everything is Vapor', 30.

[27] Gibson, *Destiny*, 15, 17.

somehow be satisfying or grant us some needed closure. Vanity infects everything, even our comprehension of vanity.

Adding insult to injury is the fact that we always want something new, something more. We cannot settle down and make peace with exhausted ennui, a low-level, half-conscious dissatisfaction. The next book, that new film, the trip we are planning – we always want something more. We are never satisfied, never full and complete and whole, never able to say 'Enough!', even when we know whatever we are looking forward to will be more of the same. It is so easy to tell ourselves, 'When I get that degree, when I get that job, when I get promoted in that job, when I marry that one special person, when we have kids . . . then, then I will be satisfied.' But we never are – and simultaneously, we are never able to suppress our desire for that next unsatisfying thing, whatever it is.

6. Conclusion and a potential objection • Ecclesiastes 1:9–11

In light of verses 2–8, verse 9 is inescapable: humanity repeats the same patterns instead of progressing. The repeating words reinforce the unbreakable repetitions of a creation subjected to frustration.

Qohelet understands that his wisdom is hard to accept, and so he anticipates a potential objection about some new idea or movement or technology or insight (verse 10). Qohelet will not allow this, however, citing faulty collective memory (verse 11): apparent innovations have been tried before, and are so buried in the forgotten mass of generations before us that we congratulate ourselves too quickly. It can be easy to dismiss this verse, of course: surely nuclear bombs or television or the moon landing or the internet are new? But all the examples that come so readily to mind are only subtypes of patterns that have continued since time immemorial: weapons, entertainment, exploration and communication are as old as humanity.[28] What seems exciting and unique to us is only a variation on a theme that has been played for millennia.

REFLECTION

Take a moment to think about the people who have lived before you – the generations who have come and gone, walking on the very soil you walk on. I'm writing this in London, which was established by the Romans around two thousand years ago. But the ancient Romans were relative newcomers. Evidence of bronze age settlements have been found here, and wider archaeological remains suggest that people have been living on this island for millennia before that. How many generations have farmed, raised families, gone to war – all the things humans do?

Going back even further, the sun has been rising and setting, the wind blowing, rivers flowing and trees dropping leaves since before this land was even an island. Now ask yourself: how much do you know about your great-grandparents? Perhaps their names? Or your great-great-grandparents?

Now imagine yourself, in the last decade of your life, at a family gathering with your grandchildren (or, if you are single, being invited to one). It's a lovely summer day and people you love are there, with lots of food and games. At one point, you get talking to these youngsters about the glory days. They sit and listen with slightly forced polite interest to how things were when you were in your prime. Soon they start fidgeting. You take the hint and tell them they can go. Off they run, squealing and chasing each other in the sunshine. They will remember some

---

[28] Fox, *A Time to Tear Down*, 168–9, appropriately compares Qohelet's view of life under the sun to a video game: the characters on screen can do different things, but the code for the game has already been written and cannot be transcended.

things about you; their own children might (might) remember your name. Nothing more.

How does that make you feel?

Qohelet has solid wisdom to offer us about living life under the sun joyfully – living in uninhibited joy, in fact. But he has given none of it to us yet, and we will not be able to receive it until, like the camel going through the eye of a needle (Matthew 19:24),[29] we allow him to undermine and expose the comforting lies we tell ourselves about why we matter and the difference we are making in the world. We will not be able to receive Qohelet's joy until we despair of our illusions. We must let him keep on pushing us until we throw up our hands and say, 'Well, what's the point of doing anything?'

It is just as well that we do. After all, we know, deep down, that all the hard things Ecclesiastes has to say are true. We squirm and our eyes dart this way and that, looking for some escape; but if we are honest, we know we leave no permanent mark on this world. Perhaps we should become more frustrated, more disappointed with life. Perhaps there are some kinds of faith we need to lose so that we can become wise. In order to hope in what does not deceive, we must first lose hope in everything that does.[30]

---

[29] Ellul draws this comparison between the reader of Ecclesiastes and the rich man who must lose everything to follow Jesus; Ellul, *Reason for Being*, 116.
[30] Ellul, *Reason for Being*, 47.

2

Qohelet's Autobiography: Three Investigations

ECCLESIASTES 1:12–2:26

Qohelet explains how he came to the understanding of life under the sun expressed in 1:2–11 by narrating three investigations which he made: life's pursuits in general (1:12–18), the best things in life (2:1–11) and wisdom itself (2:12–16). Finding that each is subject to vanity, unable to produce any lasting or permanent satisfaction, Qohelet despairs and hates life (2:17–23). But his despair is an entry into a new perspective on life under the sun as a gift from God, to be valued and enjoyed as such (2:24–6).

The crucial thing to remember in this passage is that Qohelet is narrating his past to teach us how to avoid his mistake of rejecting life (2:17) so that we can join him in his joy over God's gift (2:24).

1. First search: all human activity • Ecclesiastes 1:12–18

Wisdom is meaningless

12 I, the Teacher, was king over Israel in Jerusalem. **13** I applied my mind to study and to explore by wisdom all that is done under the heavens. What a heavy burden God has laid on mankind! **14** I have seen all the things that are done under the sun; all of them are meaningless, a chasing after the wind.

15 What is crooked cannot be straightened;
what is lacking cannot be counted.

16 I said to myself, 'Look, I have increased in wisdom more than anyone who has ruled over Jerusalem before me; I have experienced much of wisdom and knowledge.' **17** Then I applied myself to the understanding of wisdom, and also of madness and folly, but I learned that this, too, is a chasing after the wind.

18 For with much wisdom comes
   much sorrow;
   the more knowledge, the
   more grief.

Qohelet's first search (verses 12–15)

Qohelet describes his first investigation in verses 12–13, draws a conclusion in verse 14 with a reason in verse 15, and then reflects on the search itself in verses 16–18. Although it comes a bit later in the passage, his goal in each of these quests is stated in 2:3: to discover what is good for human beings in whatever time they have in this life. This is not an abstract philosophical speculation into the nature of reality; Qohelet wants to know how to live the best life.

Verse 12 repeats Qohelet's role and historical location from 1:1, and verse 16 adds that Qohelet was more accomplished than any of his predecessors. We are to imagine someone not subject to our limitations, someone who enjoys unlimited talent and resources, along with the authority to command whoever and whatever he wants. Qohelet never found himself in the position of thinking, 'If only I could do _____, then I'd be really happy.'

Furthermore, Qohelet took advantage of these talents and resources to the greatest possible extent (verse 13). Any failure in this quest was not because of any lack of care or thoroughness on his part. Qohelet applied his mind to it (literally, 'gave his heart', the heart being the core of the self in the Old Testament).[1] It was a matter of deep labour for him. The search was also done 'by wisdom', not haphazardly or superficially, but skilfully and

---

[1] *HALOT* 514–15.

insightfully. Furthermore, Qohelet investigated 'all the things that are done under the sun'. We need not imagine him investigating every single occupation in existence. Rather, he looked into all different kinds of activity. If there is something worth doing of permanent value, Qohelet would have found it.

If the reader will allow the imaginative licence, we can picture Qohelet studying political science and meeting with world leaders, then going to academic conferences and talking with philosophers and historians. He visits famous museums and studies the exhibits. He is there at CERN's Large Hadron Collider to watch them verify the existence of the Higgs boson particle. Next on his list is hearing Beethoven performed in Vienna – and then he's off to the Great Wall of China. The Pyramids are next, and then the Nazca Lines in Peru . . . and so on. All along, Qohelet takes everything in, understanding and reflecting on it all.

Despite all of Qohelet's efforts, however, there is little drama about how they will end. No sooner does he define his first search in verse 13 than he announces its failure: 'What a heavy burden God has placed on mankind!'[2] (This is the first mention of God in the book, and hardly a comforting one; let's watch for other things Qohelet will say about God later.)

Qohelet's conclusion to his first quest is that every kind of activity is *hebel* (verse 14). Our accomplishments fade quickly, failing to deliver the permanence or significance – the 'good'

---

[2] Literally, 'an evil business'. Qohelet uses the word to talk about human activity and work in general (3:10; 8:16). The adjective he uses can mean 'unhappy' or 'painful'; Antoon Schoors, *The Preacher Sought to Find Pleasing Words: A Study of the Language of Qoheleth, Part II: Vocabulary* (Leuven: Peeters, 2004), 145–52. Some commentators take this statement to be a reflection on the search itself, similar to the thought of 1:8 – for example, Fox, *A Time to Tear Down*, 171 – but Qohelet uses the word 'business' to refer to all human activity in a general sense. Qohelet's reflection on the search of verse 13 rather comes in verses 16–18.

— we want (2:3), no matter how diligently we invest ourselves in them. There is no job waiting for you which will, in itself, give you that deep satisfaction and sense of achievement and fulfilment. You are chasing after the wind. Furthermore, this is not speculation on Qohelet's part (verse 14); rather, he has seen the inability of all our different kinds of work to produce anything lasting or anything completely new.

This might seem a bit of a hasty conclusion on so broad a question – and all in just three verses. However, Qohelet provides a reason why everything that is done under the sun amounts to chasing after the wind in verse 15: there is a twistedness in things, an out-of-whack screwiness, which forever resists our attempts to straighten and order. Life simply will not serve us exactly the way we want – or, in the language of a different part of the Bible, it takes streaming sweat to get anything to grow at all, and there are always lots of weeds mixed in (Genesis 3:17–18). Not only that, there is a lack we cannot number. It is not just that we don't have all the pieces of the puzzle. We don't even know how many pieces we are missing. Little wonder, then, that control eludes us, that all our work is eventually swept away and forgotten.

Qohelet's reflection on his first search (Ecclesiastes 1:16–18)

Qohelet has defined his first quest (verse 13), stated its result (verse 14) and provided a reason for this result (verse 15). He is not quite ready to move on to his second search, however. One of the fascinating things about Qohelet is that he does not just make observations; he also observes himself observing. He thinks about his own thinking.

His first reflection of this kind comes in verses 16–18, as he inspects the wisdom by which he made his search (see verse 13). His reflection prevents any thought that it was a failure of wisdom that led to the depressing conclusion of verse 14. It was not as if reading yet one more book, or talking to more wise friends, or finding some new theory or technique, could have yielded better results and shown Qohelet something of permanent value to do. He surpassed all his predecessors in wisdom and enjoyed wisdom in abundance (verse 16). Qohelet even went so far as to examine the other side of the equation, madness and folly (verse 17). One thinks of the deliberate nonsense of absurdist movements like Dadaism – but Qohelet knows there is no answer there.

All this means it is no failure of wisdom that leads to the conclusion of verse 14, for Qohelet has wisdom in abundance, and verse 14 is still true. Even worse, the search of verses 12–14 itself, which showed every human pursuit to be chasing after the wind, is itself an example of chasing after the wind. This is not because Qohelet's conclusion is false. Rather, as in 1:8, there is no refuge from vanity in analysis of vanity. Being aware of futility is no defence against it.

The reason is given in verse 18: growing in wisdom introduces more pain into your life. Surely it is obvious that wisdom's insights into the complex but good order of God's creation should make your life better? But a moment's reflection shows that such insights will give you a clearer view of the world's brokenness as well. You will be confronted with the world's brevity, vanity and limitless absurdities, and your wisdom will take blissful ignorance away from you forever. I often tell my Oak Hill Theological College students that if their degree makes their lives easier, they should ask for their money back. For this reason, wisdom is *hebel* – pointless and absurd, because it does not repay the reasonable expectations you had for it.

2. Second search: the good life • Ecclesiastes 2:1–11

Pleasures are meaningless

2 I said to myself, 'Come now, I will test you with pleasure to find out what is good.' But that also proved to be meaningless. **2** 'Laughter,' I said, 'is madness. And what does pleasure accomplish?' **3** I tried cheering myself with wine, and embracing folly – my mind still guiding me with wisdom. I wanted to see what was good for people to do under the heavens during the few days of their lives.

4 I undertook great projects: I built houses for myself and planted vineyards. **5** I made gardens and parks and planted all kinds of fruit trees in them. **6** I made reservoirs to water groves of flourishing trees. **7** I bought male and female slaves and had other slaves who were born in my house. I also owned more herds and flocks than anyone in Jerusalem before me. **8** I amassed silver and gold for myself, and the treasure of kings and provinces. I acquired male and female singers, and a harem[a] as well – the delights of a man's heart. **9** I became greater by far than anyone in Jerusalem before me. In all this my wisdom stayed with me.

10 I denied myself nothing my eyes desired;
   I refused my heart no pleasure.
My heart took delight in all my labour,
   and this was the reward for all my toil.
11 Yet when I surveyed all that my hands had done
   and what I had toiled to achieve,
everything was meaningless, a chasing after the wind;
   nothing was gained under the sun.

---

a 8 The meaning of the Hebrew for this phrase is uncertain.

Qohelet's introduction to his second search (Ecclesiastes 2:1–3)

Having found that the world as a whole is not so wonderful, Qohelet retreats: perhaps he can quarantine himself with only the best and most enjoyable aspects of life under the sun. Perhaps he can leave the brevity and futility of things outside his palace walls. Qohelet defines this second, more focused quest in verses 1–3, already stating his conclusion at the end of verse 1 and in verse 2. Verses 4–9 detail his quest, and in verses 10–11 he states his twofold conclusion.

His second investigation begins much as his first: it is deeply careful and characterised by wisdom throughout (verse 3). We should imagine Qohelet with a glass of wine by his side as he labours over architecture plans late into the night – and if the plans are a little grandiose ('embracing folly'), what of it?[3] It is a test (verse 1), all to see what is good and worth doing (verse 3). I am reminded of C. S. Lewis's own search for joy, in which he characterised his spiritual quest as asking of each experience or pleasure, 'Is this the thing I really want? Or this?'[4]

Qohelet will not let us raise our hopes, however. Before he even fully describes his search, he tells us that it was also in vain (verse 1). A preliminary reason is given in verse 2. Have you ever been at a party where the guests seemed to be trying too hard to have fun? Where the laughter had a crazy edge to it? That is vanity seeping into even the best celebrations. Furthermore, pleasure is nice, but it doesn't accomplish anything. The five-course meal, the night at the symphony hall, the sunset enjoyed with your spouse: they are wonderful, and then they end; life clicks back to normal and you start to wonder about what's next ('The eye never has enough', Ecclesiastes 1:8). Pleasure feels nice, but it is in vain – gone too soon, and not quite giving us what we wanted.

---

[3] Alternatively, 'embracing folly' is prospective, i.e., Qohelet embraced things that turned out to be folly; Fox, *A Time to Tear Down*, 179.

[4] C. S. Lewis, *Surprised by Joy* (reprint; London: HarperCollins, 2012), 196–7, 256–7.

Qohelet's great works (Ecclesiastes 2:4–9)

As we read, perhaps a part of us is still looking for some kind of escape. Perhaps we wonder if Qohelet's imagination was not capacious enough; if we were king or queen, we would come up with something truly unforgettable. The details about the good things Qohelet gave himself to in verses 4–9 are meant to lay to rest any such thoughts.[5] From an ancient Semitic perspective, these royal accomplishments are as vast as they are impressive. All contribute to a sense of totality and completeness: Qohelet crams as much accomplishment into one life as possible. Surely, if anything counts as good for human beings to do (verse 3), if there is any gain, any permanent leftover to one's work (1:3), Qohelet has secured it. In a world of skyscrapers and laptops, of course, vineyards and gardens and pools do not sound as impressive, but the same effect of awe with a tinge of jealousy can be produced when thinking of the lives of modern billionaire entrepreneurs and celebrities.

One more thing to notice about verses 4–9 is that Qohelet says that he did all these things 'for myself' six times in as many verses (only the first is brought out clearly in the NIV).[6] At the same time, for all of Qohelet's focus on himself and his work, God is not mentioned anywhere. It is important to keep this in mind to appreciate the magnitude of Qohelet's breakthrough in 2:24–6.

---

[5] The NIV's 'harem' (verse 8) is a reasonable guess for the Hebrew *šidāh wěšidōt*. The word occurs nowhere else in Hebrew, so it is difficult to know what it means. 'Harem' or 'concubine' are possible on the basis of an Ugaritic parallel; a related verb means 'to plunder' (*šādah*) so perhaps 'captured women' is best. Alternatively, perhaps a related Aramaic verb 'to pour' (*šdy*) means that 'cupbearers' are in view. For more on this, see Weeks, *A Critical and Exegetical Commentary*, 408–13.

[6] The lamed prefix shows possession or advantage (WOC 11.2.10), so it could be translated as 'belonging to me'. However the phrase is translated, the repetition is noticeable.

Qohelet's conclusion about his second search (Ecclesiastes 2:10–11)

Qohelet reflects on this second search in verses 10–11 and draws a twofold conclusion. On the one hand, he succeeded (verse 10). He finished every item on his agenda. Not a single project was left unfinished; no desire was left unfulfilled. (What an enviable position to be in!) Not only that, Qohelet had a blast doing it all. He whistled his way to the office every morning and deeply enjoyed every project he worked on. Qohelet began this investigation by announcing his intention to test pleasure or joy (*śimḥāh*, verse 1), and ends by saying that he did not withhold any pleasure (*śimḥāh*) from his heart (verse 10). To this extent, Qohelet's search was a success.

Furthermore, Qohelet's joy in his work was his 'portion' from it (*ḥeleq*, NIV 'reward'). Elsewhere in the Old Testament, the word refers to a certain portion of spoil from battle (Genesis 14:24), one's portion of an inheritance (Genesis 31:14) or a portion of land (Numbers 18:20). This is another important word for Qohelet. More than once he will speak of our only 'portion' or 'reward' under the sun consisting in the joy we get from our work (3:22; 5:17–18; 9:9).[7] This was true for Qohelet as well: his takeaway was the delight he took in all his accomplishments. (Note that Qohelet does not say that the works themselves were his portion, but only his enjoyment of them. This will be significant as we proceed.)

On the other hand, however, Qohelet failed (verse 11). He pronounces every single one of his accomplishments from

---

[7] A former student of mine, Joshua Knowles, pointed out to me that an important aspect of Qohelet's wisdom is that we do get a 'portion' from our work in this life (our pleasure in that work), but not 'gain' (*yitrôn*, 1:3, as in something lasting and permanent). It is also worth noting in 9:6 that a 'portion' is exactly what the dead do not have, implying that the 'gain' that Qohelet wants is something that will outlive death.

verses 4–9 as *hebel*, futile. In every one of the happy hours Qohelet spent working, he was only chasing after the wind, along with the rest of humanity. In all his mighty works, he did not get any permanent gain from them (*yitrôn*, as in 1:3). This means that his very success was his failure. Qohelet didn't set his sights high and then fail to achieve his ambitions. There was nothing left undone, still in the future, for Qohelet to think, 'Maybe if I just tried that . . .' The length of the first part of the verse evokes a sense of grandeur, but it is a melancholy grandeur.

Qohelet does not give a reason why all of his successful accomplishments are in vain. The next verses, however, speak of death, so that is probably on his mind. All the senses of *hebel* seem to be in play: death renders wonderful accomplishments impermanent and thus in vain, because Qohelet wanted something from his work it did not give him. How absurd to succeed so wildly at all his ambitions, only to have the very thing Qohelet most deeply wanted all along slip out of his grasp.[8]

3. Third search: wisdom • Ecclesiastes 2:12–16

Wisdom and folly are meaningless
12 Then I turned my thoughts to
  consider wisdom,
    and also madness and folly.

What more can the king's
  successor do
    than what has already been
    done?
13 I saw that wisdom is better than

---

[8] Zach Eswine wisely makes the same point in different words. He writes of how Ecclesiastes never moves in an other-worldly direction; it never diagnoses our problem as seeking satisfaction in the wrong place. Rather, we seek satisfaction in the wrong way. Our location under the sun is not the problem, only our use of it. Looking under the sun for 'gain' in all our work simply will not work – it is not to be found here; Eswine, *Recovering Eden: The Gospel According to Ecclesiastes* (Phillipsburg: P&R, 2004), 31–2, 45.

QOHELET'S AUTOBIOGRAPHY

folly,
    just as light is better than
      darkness.
14 The wise have eyes in their
      heads,
    while the fool walks in the
      darkness;
  but I came to realise
    that the same fate overtakes
      them both.

15 Then I said to myself,
  'The fate of the fool will overtake
    me also.
  What then do I gain by being
    wise?'
I said to myself,
  'This too is meaningless.'
16 For the wise, like the fool, will
    not be long remembered;
  the days have already come
    when both have been
    forgotten.
Like the fool, the wise too must
    die!

Qohelet has searched what is good for men and women to do during their earthly lives (2:3), both in a wide-ranging way (1:12–13) and specifically with regard to the very best things in life (2:1–3). Both times, he has come up empty: there is no permanent advantage or gain in either. In light of this, Qohelet retreats further in verses 12–16. His wisdom stood with him in his first two quests as the means by which he undertook them (1:13, 16; 2:10). Now Qohelet turns to wisdom itself. Perhaps there is some permanent gain to be had here? 'Wisdom' here means both 'effective ability' and 'spiritual insight'. The first meaning is apparent in 2:9, as Qohelet skilfully brings his plans to execution (compare Exodus 28:1–3 and 31:1–6, where 'men of ability' (literally 'wisdom') build the temple furnishings). The second is apparent in the mention of light and darkness in verse 13, for these images often take on connotations of fullness of life and favour with God on the one hand, and distress and death on the other (see, for example, Proverbs 2:13; 4:18–19; 13:9; 16:15; 20:20).[9] Qohelet's third quest is a spiritual one.

---

[9] See further Seow, *Ecclesiastes*, 153. Qohelet will use the image of darkness to

We should not forget the connections to 1:2–11 at this point. Qohelet has already lamented the wearying and unbreakable patterns of activity in which humanity labours (1:4–7), in which generation after generation of work produces nothing new or lasting (the 'gain' of 1:3). He now shows us how he came to this painful insight. Gazing out over all that he has toiled to achieve, with nothing left to accomplish (verse 11), Qohelet cannot help but turn his mind to the future. He will not be around forever – but what will later kings do? Only the sorts of building projects Qohelet has spent his time on, perhaps adding to his, perhaps tearing them down and making their own (verse 12). The unavoidable conclusion is that there is nothing new under the sun, no lasting gain that can endure how the years and centuries wipe away the greatest achievements, as generations come and go, and the sun rises and sets. But Qohelet cannot rid himself of the desire for a *yitrōn* (verse 11, the same word as in 1:3), some gain or benefit that will not be wiped away by the years. So he turns to wisdom, and, as above, a paradoxical conclusion follows.

On the one hand, wisdom is in every way to be prized, in every way better than its opposite (verses 13–14a; remember that Qohelet examines both in verse 12). There is no comparison: in Old Testament wisdom literature, 'light' and 'darkness' are as absolute a contrast as can be – and not a merely theoretical one. The wise man knows how to successfully engage with life; the fool bumbles and blunders, practically and morally, and gets nowhere. Qohelet actually says there is 'gain' in wisdom more than in folly (verse 13), using the same word as in 1:3, where he denied any gain to any human activity. The 'gain' here is a relative one: wisdom is better than its opposite. But when the wide-ranging question of 1:3 is kept in mind, the bald statement of the 'gain' of wisdom is very striking.

---

talk about misery and distress (5:16) or death (6:4; 11:8; 12:2–3). 'Light' stands in opposition to both for Qohelet (11:7; 12:2).

But on the other hand, one 'fate' will happen to them all, wise and fool (14b).[10] Qohelet does not say what this 'fate' is until verse 16, but by the time we get to that verse, we have already guessed: death. We can imagine Qohelet going to the city's graveyard and standing before two graves. One is for one of his counsellors, a good friend whose counsel benefited Qohelet countless times; and not only that, this friend (let us say) also set up a charity for poor families that fed thousands. The whole city benefited from this friend's wisdom. The other grave is that of a notorious drunkard who could not hold a steady job and made life miserable for his family. He squandered life and drank himself to death.

And here they are, in the same place. What distinguishes these two, who were so obviously distinct in life? How the wise dies like the fool! Furthermore, it is a matter of time until the wind and weather wipe away the etching on their gravestones and no one remembers who they were at all (verse 16). What vanity!

I hope the reader is not here holding Qohelet's wisdom at arm's length. Have you seriously faced up to the fact that you can work with great skill at whatever God has given you to do and be of great blessing to those around you – and in the grave, you will be indistinguishable from those who wasted their lives and were a burden to those around them? Or is it one of those thoughts that is always conveniently pushed aside, unnoticed?

Please note that there is no scepticism or cynicism here. Qohelet does not conclude from this that you might as well be a fool as be wise, because nothing matters. In fact, it is just

---

[10] To whatever extent the English word 'fate' conjures up ideas of a vague, impersonal force guiding our lives, it is not a good translation, because 'fate' in that sense does not exist in the Old Testament. The word in Hebrew means something that happens independently of human planning or willpower (see Ruth 2:3; 1 Samuel 6:9). At the same time, it is hard to think of a better translation, and the connotation of some future, inescapable event fits very well with Qohelet's thought here.

because Qohelet values and prizes wisdom so highly that it vexes him so deeply that there would be no lasting reminder or recognition of it. It never occurs to him to conclude from this that anyone should give up on wisdom (a cynic's response). But from an 'under the sun' perspective – and we must never forget that Qohelet limits his investigation to what is good for human beings in this life (1:3; 2:3) – it does not matter how wise you are, or how it benefits yourself and others. You will wind up in the same place as a fool. This, also, is *hebel* (verse 15). Even so good a thing as wisdom will not give you a permanent gain under the sun.

There is one more thing to notice in verses 13–16:

The fate of the fool will overtake me also.
What then do I gain by being wise?

(The word rightly translated as 'gain' here is from the same root as *yitrôn* in 1:3, 2:13). Notice that although wisdom is good, Qohelet asked of it something it could not give him under the sun: some permanent distinction that death would not erase. When he realises this, he wonders why he bothered with it at all. His wisdom is *hebel*, 'in vain'. There is some permanent 'gain,' something not even death can erase, which Qohelet's heart wants so deeply and cannot find.

4. Qohelet despairs • Ecclesiastes 2:17–23

Toil is meaningless
17 So I hated life, because the work that is done under the sun was grievous to me. All of it is meaningless, a chasing after the wind. **18** I hated all the things I had toiled for under the sun, because I must leave them to the one who comes after me. **19** And who knows whether that person will be wise or foolish? Yet they will have control over all the fruit of my toil into which I have

poured my effort and skill under the sun. This too is meaningless. **20** So my heart began to despair over all my toilsome labour under the sun. **21** For a person may labour with wisdom, knowledge and skill, and then they must leave all they own to another who has not toiled for it. This too is meaningless and a great misfortune. **22** What do people get for all the toil and anxious striving with which they labour under the sun? **23** All their days their work is grief and pain; even at night their minds do not rest. This too is meaningless.

Qohelet has made three wise and thorough investigations into three areas of human activity under the sun, all to see what is good for us to do during our short lives (2:3) and what permanent gain we might have (2:13). Each has failed. Although he has learned that wisdom is unqualifiedly better than folly (verses 13–14a), he has found no activity or pursuit that amounts to anything more than wind-chasing, for nothing grants any kind of permanence that will outlast death. At this point, no fourth investigation is possible; he has been comprehensive in his searches. Under the sun, what else is there?

Qohelet despairs. He has come to hate both life (verse 17) and his work (verse 18). It is as if his previous achievements (verses 4–9) take on reverse meaning, mocking him and his brevity (verses 20–21). All the work he did 'for myself' now stands only as a memorial to his insignificance, not his significance. What do people get for all those years of work, Qohelet wonders (verse 22). All those years of back pain and headaches and late meetings – and then the stress bleeds into our sleep and we get no rest (verse 23). All for what? Truly, this is vanity of vanities.

Having to let go of everything he enjoyed so much is bad enough (verse 22), but salting the wound is the thought that someone else will enjoy it without lifting a finger (verses 18–21). The mere fact that this happens deeply irks Qohelet, but even worse is the thought that Qohelet cannot control whether his successor will ruin everything Qohelet has enjoyed (verse 19).

(Again: have you faced the fact that you could give fifty years of your working life to a company or ministry, and do great work, only to have your successor ruin it all in a few weeks?) The vehemence of the repeating phrases oozes bitterness: 'He will rule over all *my* labour which *I* laboured for and over which *I* was wise??!!' (verse 19, my translation).

This is Qohelet's absolute low point. For a man who loves life with such zest to tell us about how he came to hate it is sobering, to say the least. But as we will see below, despair is the gateway to joy. Indeed, there is no other way to reconcile ourselves to life under the sun without first despairing of it. Some kinds of faith are worth losing.

5. Qohelet's breakthrough • Ecclesiastes 2:24–6

24 A person can do nothing better than to eat and drink and find satisfaction in their own toil. This too, I see, is from the hand of God, **25** for without him, who can eat or find enjoyment? **26** To the person who pleases him, God gives wisdom, knowledge and happiness, but to the sinner he gives the task of gathering and storing up wealth to hand it over to the one who pleases God. This too is meaningless, a chasing after the wind.

Twice before, Qohelet has said that he sees something as he reflects on his investigations (1:14; 2:13). Now he sees something else, for which we are unprepared: there is nothing better for us to do under the sun than eat, drink and enjoy our work (verse 24). This is his final answer to the question of 2:3 (it is difficult to see in translation, but he repeats the same word 'good' twice from that earlier verse). Coming so soon after verses 17–23 – especially when Qohelet has just despaired over his 'toilsome labour' (verse 20) – it is hard to know how to take this. Is it gallows humour (compare Isaiah 22:13)? Has Qohelet simply run out of ideas? 'You might as well amuse yourself at work and then stuff yourself when you come home, because there's nothing else'?

The second line in the verse shows that Qohelet has discovered something much happier: there is nothing better for human beings than to enjoy life and work, because both are a gift from God.[11] The value of your life and work is in their status as a gift from on high, not in measurable results or any permanent gain you can win for yourself. In David Gibson's pithy formulation, life is gift, not gain.[12]

Within the context of chapter 2, we see that Ecclesiastes gives us a simple but momentous choice. On the one hand, we can work ourselves to exhaustion trying to secure for ourselves some permanent achievement through our own efforts (2:4–9), something that we can always hold on to, all the while ignoring the frustration and limitations God has imposed on creation (Romans 8:19–20, Genesis 3:19). If we take this route, we will come to hate life when it refuses to obey us (Ecclesiastes 2:17–18). On the other hand, we can deeply accept that, within the limitations of our earthly lives, we gain nothing permanent, we do not really change the world and everything slips away in the end – but God has given us today to enjoy, and each thing in it. We can accept that the only value our lives and labours have is in their status as a gift from God himself. (Remember how distant God has been in Ecclesiastes up to this point, his only mention being the imposition of that heavy burden of 1:13. Things look very different now.)

---

[11] Qohelet refers to eating and drinking, of course, not life as a whole. But in a couple of other places in the Old Testament, eating and drinking seem to represent enjoying life as a whole – especially feasting with others (see, for example, Job 1:4; Jeremiah 16:8). Especially in Ecclesiastes, eating and drinking seem to stand as part-for-whole for enjoying all of life, as if we never do so more fully than when feasting with friends.

[12] Gibson repeats this in *Destiny*, e.g., 32–4, 55.

This means that whatever time you spend reading the book you are holding right now, and whatever you do after you put this book down – be it as momentous as addressing Parliament or as humdrum as putting out the rubbish – is given to you by God. You will get nothing permanent from it. Eventually you will die, and everyone who ever knew you will die, and the world will grind on regardless, and whatever mark you made on the world will be wiped away, and it will be as if you never existed. Eventually the book you hold will be forgotten, relegated to second-hand bookshops, and finally thrown away, and other commentaries will take its place, and new generations of readers will puzzle their heads over Ecclesiastes. (The sun rises, the sun sets, the earth stands forever.) But God himself, in his infinite providence, as he guides all the vast minutiae of his world, across millennia of human history: he has decided to give you personally the next quarter of an hour to sit in your favourite chair, read this book, reflect and be his creature under the sun. That is a good thing.

But not everything. Qohelet phrases his wisdom as 'better than', i.e., better than hating and rejecting life. But this is not an absolute good. The wisdom of 2:24 is a workable strategy for living with *hebel*, not a master plan to subjugate existence.[13] This is because even receiving life as a gift is subject to *hebel*. God's earthly gifts of life, eating with our friends, work that we find interesting and so on are still futile. Each is gone all too soon, and none of them is quite what we wanted. In other words, Qohelet is not recommending enjoyment as a way of sneaking

---

[13] In a helpful article, R. K. Johnston traces how Qohelet repeatedly describes something as *hebel*, recommends enjoying life as an alternative and then qualifies his recommendation, implying that such enjoyment does not deliver us from *hebel* or give us a way to master life. Since God has placed such mastery out of our reach, there is nothing better than simply taking each good thing as it comes; Johnson, '"Confessions of a Workaholic": A Reappraisal of Qoheleth', *Catholic Biblical Quarterly* 38 (1976): 14–28, especially 21.

permanent gain in through the back door, as if following the book's wisdom will let us escape life's frustrations. Qohelet's whole point is that life is both good and in vain — a gift entire, but forever subject to *hebel*. Neither cancels the other.[14]

In fact, there is a sense in which we need *hebel* before we can accept life as a gift. The brevity and vanity of life only make it unlivable if we try to control it. Once we despair and give up seeking to gain anything permanent, *hebel* becomes the context within which we can open our hands and accept each thing as a gift directly from our Creator. Life becomes something we receive instead of something we master. But I do not think any of us will be able to stop grasping and simply receive until we have wrestled with the world's vanity and been defeated. Something wonderful happens after this defeat: the very thing about life that used to drive us crazy allows us to enjoy it, for however long God gives it — and to go our way with peace when he stops. 'In order to hope in what does not deceive, we must first lose hope in everything that does,' as Ellul puts it.[15]

What I find mindboggling about Qohelet's wisdom, and what makes me so grateful for it, is the way he forces me to confront all the things I intuitively think would make me hate life (my own insignificance and impending death), and then helps me see that these are actually the context within which I can receive life as a gift. With Qohelet as my guide, all the things I try to avoid deliver me into a place where I can enjoy life; not only that, they also bring me close to God the great Giver.

Qohelet's insight is the best way to engage with life I have ever read, even in Christian books, whether academic or practical. Qohelet returns to it more than once, and we will reflect with him each time he does (see 3:12–13, 22; 5:18–20; 8:15; 9:7–9; 11:1–6).

---

[14] Ellul, *Reason for Being*, 31.
[15] Ellul, *Reason for Being*, 47. See further Gibson's striking formulation of this in *Destiny*, 23–4, 31.

But for now, let us finish the chapter by turning to verses 25–26, where Qohelet gives us two further reasons to enjoy life as God's gift. The first is that it is only by God's gift that anyone can enjoy life (verse 25). We are not sovereign over our own existences (see 6:2; 7:13–14), so it is foolish to refuse divine gifts we cannot secure for ourselves. A further reason to enjoy life comes in verse 26: God orders the patterns of creation such that those who please him receive the efforts of others. Pleasing God is very general, of course, but in context it especially refers to those who surrender to *hebel* and receive life as a gift, as opposed to sinners who live for themselves, as if God is not there. Qohelet was earlier bothered at the thought of someone else enjoying what he worked for (verse 21); now he sees how those who fear God are actually in that very position. This, too, is *hebel* (verse 26), because there is 'an asymmetry between effort and result'.[16] But God can spin *hebel* in our favour. His gifts have a way of multiplying.[17]

REFLECTION

One of the things I enjoy most is getting up early and drinking coffee as I read my Bible and try to pray. I have a mug which a Canadian friend made on his own pottery wheel. It's pleasant to the touch and fits snugly in my hand. It's lovely to have something that wakes me up (at the time of writing, I am forty-six and feeling every inch of it). The smell, the little eddy of steam

---

[16] Fox, *A Time to Tear Down*, 191.

[17] A number of very wise readers of Ecclesiastes claim that the 'sinner' in this verse is emptied of any moral content and only means someone 'unlucky', because Qohelet elsewhere denies the doctrine of retribution (i.e., the idea taught in Proverbs that good and bad people each reap what they sow). In other words, the two categories of people in this verse are only inexplicably lucky and unlucky people; see Fox, *A Time to Tear Down*, 189–90; Seow, *Ecclesiastes*, 141. I do not find this convincing because, although Qohelet is mystified by the timing and execution of God's judgment, he does not deny the doctrine (8:12–13). He also speaks of sinners in moral categories in 5:5 and 7:20.

that rises as the house is dark and quiet and I read . . . for such a small thing, I find it very pleasant.

Certainly, I get no permanent benefit from coffee. It tastes good and then it's gone, and eventually I want more. ('What does pleasure accomplish? The eye is never satisfied with seeing . . .') But Qohelet teaches me that, although this pleasure is a very impermanent one, it is not random. God gave it to me to drink coffee from my favourite mug this morning.

Let's think about this for a moment. Pottery is incalculably old; the world's earliest ceramics date back tens of thousands of years. But at some point, someone living long ago takes a break from working in his field to watch his child making shapes in the mud. After a while the child runs off to play somewhere else, and the man sees that the shapes his son made are hardening as the clay dries in the hot sun. He thinks to himself, 'Huh. I wonder what would happen if I put that in an oven.' It works; the technique is refined and spreads around the world.

Many years later, someone in the forests of Ethiopia crushes a dark bean from a tall bushy plant and experiments with drinking it in hot water – and starts to feel very alert and happy. He invites over a friend; eventually the coffee trade spreads through Europe – and now I have coffee each morning, in a mug my friend made for me.[18]

Consider: in God's mindboggling guidance of all human history, one of the reasons that ancient farmer invented pottery, and one of the reasons that Ethiopian experimented with a coffee bean, was so that Eric Ortlund could enjoy a cup of coffee in London, England, in 2024. God orchestrated the vast sea of history for countless reasons – but one of them was so that I could take those sips, from my favourite mug, in my favourite chair.

---

[18] I am grateful to my father, Ray Ortlund, for helping me see this passage this way, in a sermon on Ecclesiastes preached on 2 August 2020 at Immanuel Church in Nashville, Tennessee.

How does that make you look at drinking coffee differently? Does God seem different to you?

Let's apply this to non-trivial pleasures. Think about that big project at work you are genuinely excited to sink your teeth into; or the child who needs steering through that next stage of life; that novel you always told yourself you'd write which you finally started; or (if you're in ministry), that new sermon series, or the camp you're going to lead, or the building project you're going to spearhead. God himself, the Almighty Sovereign and your heavenly Father, has guided the uncountable millennia of sunrises and sunsets, generations that have come and gone, come and gone, all so that you can engage with this particular task. (Consider, too, how many people had to meet and fall in love and have children, just so that you could exist.) It is his gift, directly from him, personally to you. How many others have laboured (many unknown to you) so that you can do today's tasks – some of them living in defiance of their Creator (2:26)? And when you think about all this, how does tomorrow's time at the office look different?

You will gain nothing permanent from this work. Even if your company puts a plaque of you on the wall with your picture, everyone at your company will forget who you are eventually; you'll just be a name. Indulge in the illusion of control and when it comes time to retire, you'll be stressed and frustrated at how those young bloods are messing with your work, or perhaps ruining it. Even within your life, everything you work on will slip out of your hands. The only thing you keep is the enjoyment you had while you worked (remember 2:10). Nevertheless, whatever you do in the next hour is a gift from God, directly to you: talking to that client, working on that project, designing that presentation, redecorating that room or writing that sermon.

David Gibson puts it this way: once we accept the brevity of our lives and achievements, we learn to enjoy good things in life without expecting too much from them, receiving them:

... for what they are in themselves, rather than what we need them to be to make us happy ... Instead of using these gifts as means to a greater end of securing ultimate gain in the world, we take the time to live inside the gifts themselves and see the hand of God in them ... What if our work was never intended to make us successful, but simply to make us faithful and generous?[19]

In other words, life 'is meant to be enjoyed, not mastered'.[20]

The issue can be put this way: every human being has the choice to work either for visible results or for God. Make the first your goal and you will either have to lie to yourself about how quickly you are gone, or you will burn out chasing after the wind and start hating your life. Make the latter your goal and you are delivered from being important or influential, and you will be in a position simply to receive each thing as a gift.[21] This delivers us from the mistake of either thinking that our time on this planet is our one chance to create a perfect life for ourselves or thinking that life is a sadistic joke, meant to break our hearts.[22]

Think about the morning or afternoon's tasks, and about the useless gifts that they are. Before God's holy presence, talk through how each one is in vain, and also a good gift from heaven. I find this practice sanity-restoring; it helps me to feel settled, calm, happy. Ecclesiastes has an understandable reputation for being depressing, but I find it liberating. The book is certainly not easy: Qohelet is trying to shatter comforting illusions which

---

[19] Gibson, *Destiny*, 31–3.

[20] Gibson, *Destiny*, 33.

[21] We will get into this in 7:15–18, but I do not think it is wrong to associate the language of gift in Ecclesiastes with grace in the New Testament. The proportion of thought seems the same: God gives, irrespective of accomplishment/works.

[22] I am thankful to my father, Ray Ortlund, for this insight (private communication).

most cling to about life under the sun. But if I allow him to do so, Qohelet helps me stop worrying about the results of my work or what kind of mark I am making on the world, all of which are out of my control anyway. Instead of fretting over results, I can take each half-hour as a gift from God, and leave the results with him. I don't know what will come from this day's work, but I can enjoy it as a gift. What a relief!

3

Everything Beautiful in Its Time

ECCLESIASTES 3:1–15

The nature of the order God has imposed on life under the sun is clarified. God has appointed the different times and seasons in which we live (verses 1–8), but also puts an impulse within our hearts towards eternity which can never be fully satisfied (verse 11). God does this to drive us to himself (verse 14). In light of our awkward position within time but yearning for the eternal, Qohelet recommends the enjoyment of this present life as a divine gift (verses 12–13).

The key to this passage is to remember that it reflects not a change in Qohelet's teaching, but his reconciliation with God's imposition of brevity and limitation on created life (1:2–11) in light of his insight about life as a divine gift (2:24–6).

After the catalogue of appropriate times for action (verses 1–8), Qohelet explores God's purpose in his ordering of time and how to live well within it as a chiasm:

A) No permanent profit (verses 9–10)
B) God's strange work of ordering human life incomprehensible to humans (verse 11)
C) Nothing better than to enjoy life as a gift from God (verses 12–13)
B') God's strange work of ordering human existence unchangeable by humans (verse 14)
A') Nothing new under the sun (verse 15)

1. A time for everything • Ecclesiastes 3:1–8

A time for everything

3 There is a time for everything,
and a season for every activity under the heavens:

2 a time to be born and a time to die,
a time to plant and a time to uproot,
3 a time to kill and a time to heal,
a time to tear down and a time to build,
4 a time to weep and a time to laugh,
a time to mourn and a time to dance,
5 a time to scatter stones and a time to gather them,
a time to embrace and a time to refrain from embracing,
6 a time to search and a time to give up,
a time to keep and a time to throw away,
7 a time to tear and a time to mend,
a time to be silent and a time to speak,
8 a time to love and a time to hate,
a time for war and a time for peace.

This beautiful passage is well-known on its own, outside the flow of Ecclesiastes as a whole. When read against the futility and dreariness of the passing generations of 1:2–11, however, it becomes even more moving. Instead of the weary, oppressive repetition of empty time in 2:4–11, a harmony emerges under God's hand of appropriate times for different actions.[1] This order is both intimate and vast: specific actions each have their right time, but the contrasting pairs suggest a sense of totality (an appropriate time for every kind of activity in life).

Qohelet is not surrendering any of the claims he made about *hebel* in chapter 1. 'A time to' implies that humanity cannot

---

[1] The infinitives in verses 1–8 are obligatory/gerundival, 'a time that ____ should be done' (WOC 36.2.3).

choose these different times, only respond to what meets them. Nor is there any discernible order or pattern in these times: one situation after another meets us, and who knows what tomorrow will bring (compare 7:14)? Furthermore, the action appropriate to certain times may be very unpleasant: weeping (verse 4), or even war (verse 8).[2] We still exist under the sun, subject to limitations not of our choosing. God orders our lives without consulting us or asking our opinion.

Despite all this, a tone of relief and release is almost palpable in these verses (in fact, he does not use the word *hebel* at all in this passage). Having accepted the blessed defeat of receiving life as God's gift instead of trying to gain permanent significance through personal achievement, Qohelet is able to view life under the sun in a whole new way: beautiful instead of oppressive. Accepting earthly life as God's gift changes everything.

2. Enjoyment within limitation • Ecclesiastes 3:9–15

9 What do workers gain from their toil? **10** I have seen the burden God has laid on the human race. **11** He has made everything beautiful in its time. He has also set eternity in the human heart; yet[a] no one can fathom what God has done from beginning to end. **12** I know that there is nothing better for people than to be happy and to do good while they live. **13** That each of them may eat and drink, and find satisfaction in all their toil – this is the gift of God. **14** I know that everything God does will endure for ever; nothing can be added to it and nothing taken from

---

[2] It is not entirely clear to me what gathering and scattering stones refers to, beyond creating/organising or pulling something apart (verse 5). For a list of options, see C. L. Seow, *Ecclesiastes*, 161. Qohelet is doubtless speaking in generalities in each of these verses ('to embrace' in the next line covers many different kinds of embracing). In my opinion, the ambiguity is pleasingly evocative.

it. God does it so that people will fear him.

15 Whatever is has already been,
and what will be has been before;
and God will call the past to account.^b

---

a 11 Or *also placed ignorance in the human heart, so that*
b 15 Or *God calls back the past*

Still no gain (verses 9–10)

Significant echoes to chapter 1 continue in verses 9–10. The question of verse 9 is practically identical to Qohelet's fundamental question about life from 1:3. The answer has not changed: we get no (permanent) gain as we move through the different seasons of verses 1–8. Furthermore, verse 10 almost perfectly echoes 1:13–14, as a more woodenly literal translation shows:

> It is an evil business God has given to the sons of men to be busy in. I have seen all the works which are done under the sun . . . (1:13–14)

> I have seen the business which God has given to the sons of men to be busy in (3:10)

The key difference between the two sets of verses is that Qohelet does not repeat that this business is 'evil' (*ra'*; in context, 'unhappy, unfortunate'). We still get nothing permanent out of life – but this does not frustrate Qohelet as it used to. Qohelet can affirm that the different seasons and activities of life are beautiful (verse 11), even as they slip away from him forever.

Eternity in their heart (verse 11)

A good deal of verses 9–15 cover the same ground as 1:2–11 from the new perspective of 2:24. We have already seen how this is the case for verses 9–10, and soon verses 12–13 will return to Qohelet's central strategy about dealing with *hebel* which he gained at the end of chapter 2. Before doing so, however, we are given a stunning insight into God's ordering of creation after the fall and before the eschaton. Three claims are made.

First, God has made everything beautiful in its time. Life under the sun is still brief, futile, subject to all kinds of distortions; but it need not be hateful. As at other points, we see the 'bothness' to Qohelet's wisdom: utterly in vain, and also beautiful.

Second, God has put 'eternity in the human heart'. We should see a contrast between ordinary earthly time in the prior clause and something beyond time here.[3] As we enjoy the different seasons of life, we have a God-given impulse towards something that transcends the seasons. God beautifies the passing seasons of our lives, but will not let us settle down and get comfortable within them. Life under the sun, good as it is, is never enough. God will not let it be. Although it remains hidden in the background, I think this explains the frustration driving 1:2–11, and Qohelet's desire for something permanent or enduring (a desire that lives in each human heart).[4]

Third, God simultaneously frustrates this impulse towards eternity. Journeying through the different seasons of life from within, we yearn for something that transcends these individual times, some comprehensive, bird's-eye view of the whole of reality

---

[3] The word in Hebrew (*'ōlām*) can mean 'a long time', 'the distant past or future' (as in Ecclesiastes 1:10; 2:16), or something like 'perpetuity' or 'everlasting', e.g., the earth stands 'for ever' in 1:4; the grave is humanity's 'eternal' home in 12:5. 'Eternity' in the sense of that which transcends earthly time is often elsewhere not the best translation, but is appropriate here because of the contrast with (earthly) time in the previous clause; Seow, *Ecclesiastes*, 163.

[4] The NIV's footnote about 'ignorance' as an alternate translation is possible but less preferable. Qohelet certainly does teach that we are ignorant of the totality of God's work in all creation (8:17), but without eternity in the human heart, it is difficult to understand why this bothers us.

and God's work in all things. God has given us this yearning – but also blocks our view of it. We are haunted by that sweetly maddening sense of some vast significance, just beyond our reach. We know God is at work in everything, but we simply cannot see how.

Enjoying life as a gift (verses 12–13)

It is natural to ask, at this point, why God would put humanity in so awkward a position between time and eternity. Qohelet has an answer (verse 14), but he first returns to his central insight about the wisest way to negotiate life under the sun: enjoy life and work as a gift from God. As in chapter 2, this is not everything ('nothing better for people than . . .'). It does not unlock life's mysteries or give us control over our lives. But not even the echoing eternity in the human heart changes our creaturely position of needing to accept each day and its labours from God. We do not sovereignly create or guide our own lives; we only receive.

Note that such joyful reception involves doing good (verse 12). Qohelet's recommendation of joy is not selfish, for charity is a part of it. Note as well how 'democratic' these pleasures are, especially in view of Qohelet's accomplishments in 2:4–9. Only a very few human beings will enjoy the resources to engage in the sorts of projects Qohelet did, but anyone can eat and drink, be generous and enjoy their work. Furthermore, Qohelet makes no distinction between different kinds of work. You might be a janitor or work in a call centre; you might be a brain surgeon or international diplomat. It does not matter. Your work is valuable because God has given it to you to do. This prevents any arrogance on the part of well-paid professionals over and against manual labour, as if medicine or law were more important than being a plumber – and it also prevents anyone from treating manual labour as if it were 'real work', as opposed to that of philosophers or research scientists.[5] All kinds of work are equally valuable to God, equally gifts from him.

Furthermore, Qohelet says he knows this (verse 12). It is not a guess or a shot in the dark. There is nothing else for us but to receive from God and enjoy.

Fearing and trusting God (verses 14–15)

Very unlike human labours, God's work is both permanent and enduring; no one and nothing apart from him can frustrate or change his purposes (i.e., nothing can be added or taken from it). Qohelet repeatedly insists that God is intimately at work in everything, and that his work from eternity is entirely free from the frustrations and limitations he places on the created sphere (e.g., 8:17). Particularly in this context, however, it is God's work in verse 11 that is unalterable: we cannot change or affect how he beautifies each season but prevents us from losing ourselves in them by putting an unsatisfied desire for eternity in our heart.

We also learn that his ultimate purpose in doing so is that we will fear him (verse 14); that is, revere and trust him as God and Lord, who does not consult us. The fear of the Lord here should be understood in the same way as in passages like Psalm 2:11–12; Proverbs 1:7; 3:6–7; or Deuteronomy 10:12–13. This is not cowering before a tyrant, but is part and parcel with loving, trusting and obeying God. This is extremely significant: God imposes *hebel* on creation to drive us to himself, as God and Lord.

Let us consider our position as human beings from the perspective of Ecclesiastes 3:11–14. On the one hand, God does not abandon us to empty drudgery, as Qohelet experienced in chapter 1. He orders our lives beautifully within time, and gives us assurance deep within that there is something more – some

---

[5] Christopher Watkin, *Thinking Through Creation: Genesis 1 and 2 as Tools of Cultural Critique* (Phillipsburg: P&R, 2017), 111–14.

transcendent reality, not subject to the mysteries, the decay, the disorders of life under the sun. But strain as we might, we can never reach it. It is a severe kindness: if God did not impose these limitations, if we could establish some permanent significance through our own accomplishments, would any of us take God seriously? (Remember how little Qohelet said about God in chapters 1–2.) How easy it would be, without the limitations of brevity and vanity, to treat God as a business partner, relating to him only to the extent that he fits within our life projects. The gracious intent behind God's imposition of *hebel* on creation is similar to his blocking access to the tree of life in the garden (Genesis 3:24) or limiting man's life span (Genesis 6:3) or confusing human language (Genesis 11:6–7): although the results are tragic, his purpose is to keep us from sinning in ever more grotesque ways and to turn us to himself.

From this perspective, vanity and brevity become an opportunity to accept our role as creatures and receive everything from our Creator. They also show a striking picture of grace: once we understand God's motive in imposing brevity and vanity on creation of driving us to himself, together with the call to enjoy our useless lives as gifts, we realise that God graciously gives to us the lives we would otherwise abuse as opportunities for self-investment and self-promotion. In a strange way, it is the best of both worlds: God takes away from earthly life what would otherwise be spiritually dangerous for us, while still giving us those lives to enjoy.

God is not really giving us a choice. We see this in verse 15: God imposes repeating patterns on human life which we cannot affect or alter. Qohelet's reconciliation to life under the sun does not change our fundamental position of being caught in these unalterable repeating patterns of life (see 1:9–10). But just as in verse 14, Qohelet adds a tantalising insight about life under the sun. The NIV's 'God will call the past to account' over-translates a more enigmatic phrase: 'God seeks what is pursued.'[6] Qohelet does not elaborate on exactly what is being pursued, or what it means that God seeks it. But Qohelet was pursuing a lot of things in chapter 2, and humanity as a whole chases things like the ceaseless wind of 1:6. Would it be too much to suggest that God cares for and holds safe all the things we pursue but cannot hold on to?[7] That all the things which slip from our grasp are kept safe, and we will meet them again? The clause is so brief that it is difficult to be sure, but this would certainly fit with other parts of Ecclesiastes, and the Bible as a whole.

It is easy to agree with David Gibson when he writes on this verse that he is 'very glad' that 'God will one day call back and seek out' parts of his past, because 'my story has broken characters, jarring interruptions, unexpected joys, relationships caught up in unresolved tensions and difficulties, [and] unexplained contradictions'.[8] If we were the sole author of our lives, what a poor patchwork our stories would be! But our Creator both beautifies our earthly chapters (verse 11) and will one day draw them together into a harmony we cannot presently imagine.

REFLECTION
A strange and strangely moving view of life under the sun emerges from Ecclesiastes 3:1–15. One the one hand, all the severities of chapter 1 are present: God imposes an intractable vanity on our lives as we live within repeating patterns we cannot change (verses 14a, 15a), busy with work (verse 10) which

---

[6] Qohelet does not use the second verb elsewhere, and the only other example of the Niphal of this verb is found in Lamentations 5:5, where it means 'to be hunted'.

[7] Another interpretation would be that God 'seeks what is pursued', inasmuch as he keeps things in the same patterns, without letting anything slip away; i.e., the last part of the verse reinforces the first; Weeks, *A Critical and Exegetical Commentary*, 508; similarly Fox, *A Time to Tear Down*, 213–14.

[8] Gibson, *Destiny*, 47.

ultimately gives us nothing (verse 9). On the other hand, enjoying the most ordinary of tasks and meals is not just possible, but commanded (verses 12–13). Dare we refuse God's very gifts? Not only that, the different seasons of our lives – times we can only respond to, not pick and choose – are beautiful (verses 1–8, 11). The absence of any weariness or frustration as Qohelet regards the same realities of vanity he described in chapter 1 is very striking. That is how much of a difference the insight into life as a divine gift makes.

And beyond this, two hints of above-the-sun eternity touch life under the sun, like shafts shining from we know not where, but lighting up our whole journey: eternity in our hearts (verse 11), and God seeking what we chase but can never hold on to (verse 15). Beneath the hum and humdrum of work and meetings and sleep and weekends, the awareness of something beyond the immediate lies deep within. What it is, we cannot say. We are assured that God is profoundly at work in each moment of our lives, infinitely beyond the limitations he imposes on creation. But we simply cannot see what he is doing (verse 11). Not only that, God keeps safe everything that slips away from us. These things are not lost forever. We will meet them again, when the spirit returns to God (12:7) and we stand before God's good judgment (12:14) – and we will finally see what God was up to in the ordinariness of our lives, and what our lives really meant.

In Ecclesiastes, these are only hints. It is appropriate that they remain so within this book, for Qohelet understands how easy it is to use even scriptural truth as a shield against the hard realities of a frustrated creation. At the same time, I hope the reader is not unduly discouraged at this point. The judgment for 'good' in Ecclesiastes 12:14 is the book's version of the 'well done' to those faithful servants who finally stand before Christ at the end of the age (Matthew 25:21). God is intimately at work in all things, and our ordinary lives matter deeply to him – so much so that unspeakable joys are promised to those who serve him now.

The final chapter of this book confirms what other biblical books teach. But particularly in Ecclesiastes, serving God well and faithfully in this age means submitting and conforming to God's ordering of our lives, keeping the earthly vanity of our work and ministries forever before us and leaving the heavenly results of our work entirely in God's hands. This is the book's wisdom. Remembering vanity lets God be God and is a powerful antidote to any idolatry of work, any presumption that we are erecting great memorials to ourselves. This is true even if – especially if – we serve in full-time ministry. Remembering God's purpose in imposing frustration on creation also prevents us from resenting a God who gives us decades of wearying labour without anything permanent to show for them in this life. Receiving earthly life as a gift lets it be what it is: a good thing, but not everything.

It bears repeating: your life and work, whatever you do, is a gift of God, not an opportunity for you to make a name for yourself. Whether you are looking forward to your job tomorrow or dreading it, it is something God is giving to you to do. It matters, but not because of anything you accomplish, and nothing you produce on your own will redeem all the long hours and years you spend at the office. Your life is valuable for one reason only: God has given it to you. So rejoice in it, do good to others, eat and drink with your family, and leave safe with God the days that slip away from you (verse 15). For this is precisely Qohelet's paradox: only after we surrender our attempt to master our lives can we really engage with them. Qohelet's wisdom is one of defeated reception, and it is the only way to avoid hating life under the sun or lying to ourselves about it.

Furthermore, we must never forget God's ultimate purpose in imposing frustration and brevity on creation: to pry us away from playing God for ourselves and to drive us to himself in reverent trust (verse 14). Everything Qohelet found wearying and frustrating in 1:2–11 is actually meant for our spiritual good.

God has created the best sort of environment for us to learn to treat him as God and Lord.

Finally, do not deny or suppress those hints of eternity that niggle and nag through the day. You will never completely understand, never quite get to the bottom of that inarticulable sense of something more – some eternal springtime, sharp and brilliant as snow and warm as a summer's day, forever rich as autumn and forever new as spring. God is keeping you from getting too comfortable with the good things he gives you, reminding you of that day when the sun you labour under will fall from the sky and you will stand face to face with your Creator.

4

Oppression

ECCLESIASTES 3:16–22

In light of the amazing brutality of human beings and our quickly approaching demise, do not make your enjoyment of your work dependent on some future circumstance.

Ecclesiastes 1:2–3:15 fit together well as Qohelet's diagnosis of the human condition as vanity (1:2–11), a narrative of how he reached this conclusion (1:12–2:26) and a redescription of the same in light of Qohelet's reconciliation to that life. Until the climax of 11:1–12:7, Qohelet moves from one situation to the next, teaching us wisdom about negotiating *hebel* as he does. He considers injustice first.

16 And I saw something else under the sun:

> in the place of judgment –
>> wickedness was there,
> in the place of justice –
>> wickedness was there.

17 I said to myself,

> 'God will bring into judgment
>> both the righteous and the wicked,
> for there will be a time for every activity,
>> a time to judge every deed.'

18 I also said to myself, 'As for humans, God tests them so that they may see that they are like the animals. **19** Surely the fate of human beings is like that of the animals; the same fate awaits them both: as one dies, so dies the other. All have the same breath[c]; humans have no advantage over animals. Everything is meaningless. **20** All go to the same place; all come from dust, and to dust all return. **21** Who knows if the human spirit rises upward and if the spirit of the animal goes down into the earth?'

22 So I saw that there is nothing better for a person than to enjoy their work, because that is their lot. For who can bring them to see what will happen after them?

---

c 19 Or *spirit*

1. Injustice judged • Ecclesiastes 3:16–17

This is not the last time that Qohelet will observe injustice, and he will reserve the strongest language for later passages. But verse 16 is still meant to hurt: it is not just the presence of injustice that he sees, but the violation of justice in the very place where justice should be done. The vulnerable and needy are disadvantaged, and the very judges appointed to defend them instead defraud and cheat them.

But Qohelet is not a sceptic. He is convinced that God will judge every injustice and restore the victims of injustice (divine judgment in the Old Testament involves both punishment and reward). The reference to 'time' in the second half of verse 17 echoes the same word in 3:1–8: just as God organises the different seasons of our lives without consulting us, so he will inescapably deal with every injustice ever committed, whether in this life or the next. Recognising and accepting the brevity and futility of our lives does not take this assurance from us.[1]

---

[1] The Hebrew of verse 17 actually ends with the word 'there', probably referring to the courtroom where justice was violated in verse 16. That is the very place God deals with it.

OPPRESSION

2. God's searching test and levelling judgment • Ecclesiastes 3:18–21

The relationship between verses 16–17 and 18–21 is not entirely clear to me, because Qohelet says nothing further about injustice or God's judgment of it in verses 18–21, and because the Hebrew of verse 18 is a bit difficult to make sense of.[2] But it appears that verses 18–21 explore further God's purposes in both allowing injustice and eventually judging it. The connection with verse 17 seems to be that the beastly and brutal behaviour (verse 18) which these injustices perpetuate is meant to show us clearly which side of the infinite distance between Creator and creature we belong to: in comparison to God, we are in the same category as animals, as our behaviour sometimes proves. (This does not deny the special privilege humanity enjoys of bearing God's image; it only confirms the ubiquitous scriptural teaching of the abyss between Creator and creation.) It may also be that the judgment of God from verse 17 is in the background of verse 18. If this is the case, the point is the same: both God's local interventions in justice and the final reckoning and account we each must render to God show who is God and who is not.

Verses 19–21 give the reason why what God shows us in verse 18 is true: there is no distinction between animal and human death. The same fate happens to us all, and humans have no benefit or advantage over animals in death. A helpful Old Testament parallel here is Psalm 104:29–30, where God's gathering of his Spirit returns all life back to the dust, while that same Spirit shed abroad brings new life to all creation. Both passages put human beings in the larger category of 'creation',

---

[2] The Hebrew of this line is difficult, literally: 'I said in my heart concerning the sons of man, "God to test and to see that they are a beast, even they, to themselves."' A finite verb seems to have dropped out. The NIV's rendering adequately communicates the best sense we can make of the verse.

87

utterly dependent on God for our existence. Without denying what is unique about human beings, that is still basically where we stand before God.

This is one of several points where the Christian reader will be most likely to throw up their hands and dismiss Qohelet as an unbeliever: surely it is just in the transition from this life to the next, to be in Christ's presence forevermore, that we are *least* like animals? Two things are helpful to remember here. First, Qohelet does not deny an above-the-sun perspective and a reunion with our Creator after death (12:7; compare 12:14). Second, his focus is on life under the sun. If we limit ourselves in the same way, the glorious promises of the resurrection and the life of the world to come do not mitigate the fact that physical death can be as ugly and senseless as roadkill. Unpleasant as it is, we must let Qohelet puncture our illusions. Imagine a fatal car accident involving a saintly believer, a friend who is a staunch atheist and the family dog. Is there any obvious difference between the three bodies that the rescue services find? 'All come from dust, and to dust all return' (verse 20) – just as Genesis 3:19 teaches. This is fortunately not the only thing the Bible has to say about death, but it is one of the things God's word teaches us, and the wise take it to heart (see 7:2).

The question of verse 21 can be read along these lines. Instead of a denial of life after death in God's presence, the 'who knows' can be a way of asking, 'Can anyone point to any obvious difference in how humans die, in contrast to animal death – the physical process of dying – which unambiguously points to the soul's reception by God in eternity?' (I, for one, cannot.) On the other hand, Qohelet shows a progression of thought in his book. It could be that, at this early stage, he is genuinely in doubt about the spirit's return to God, only to resolve that doubt with certainty that 'the spirit returns to God who gave it' (12:7). The Bible is patient with doubt (Jude 22); if this is the right way to understand this verse, we can be similarly patient with Qohelet.

OPPRESSION

3. Enjoy life now • Ecclesiastes 3:22

Qohelet continually returns to his basic strategy for dealing with life under the sun: to enjoy it. This pleasure is not absolute or perfect, but there is nothing better for us. Two reasons are given for doing so (in addition to the fact that it is God's gift, as other passages of this kind teach). First, it is our 'lot'. This is the same word as 'reward' at the end of 2:10; although Qohelet denies any permanent, enduring gain from work, he does allow us a reward – the fun we have in working. That is the only thing we take away from it.

The second reason for enjoying our work is that we do not know what the future will bring. This is, of course, true in a general sense. But in context, Qohelet may be thinking of future injustices we suffer that are not immediately rectified (verses 16–17) or that final return to the dust which awaits us all (verse 20). You could be wrongfully terminated tomorrow. You might die in your sleep this evening. You just do not know. So enjoy your work now. You may have to say goodbye to it sooner than you think.

REFLECTION
William Shakespeare once wrote that 'security is mortals' chiefest enemy'.[3] Qohelet certainly allows us little security in this difficult passage. He will not let us look away from deeply entrenched injustice which corrupts the very place justice is supposed to be enacted, or that final end coming to us all, no different (from an 'under-the-sun' perspective) from that of animals. As a commentator, I certainly would not want to take away a single one of those 'great and precious promises' (2 Peter 1:4) which both Testaments give believers, as we face both injustices in this life and God's judgment of every human being. At the same

---
[3] William Shakespeare, *Macbeth*, act 3, scene 5.

time, we must let Qohelet expose our tendency to sugarcoat or sentimentalise death, even a saint's death. Qohelet will not allow us any Promethean pride or presumption about our ability to redress the wrongs of this life ('that they may see that they are like the animals', verse 18) – or that final appointment which God has set for every individual (Hebrews 9:27). 'The heart of the wise is in the house of mourning' (7:4). As A. B. Caneday writes:

> Witness how people, even Christians, repress grief and sorrow. Euphemisms mute grim reality. Even for Christians, funerals have become celebrations of the deceased rather than ceremonies of mourning the death of a loved one. For it is unnerving and distressing to come face to face with the pervasiveness, perversity, and profundity of the curse with which the Creator inflicted his own creation on account of human rebellion.[4]

We will never truly be able to embody verse 22 until we follow Qohelet and other wise men to the house of mourning. We will never appreciate our work so much as when we keep in mind those unredressed injustices that destroy lives, and that final enemy which destroys each life at last. 'Frustration is better than laughter, because a sad face is good for the heart' (7:3).

---

[4] A. B. Caneday, '"Everything Is Vapor:" Grasping for Meaning under the Sun,' *Southern Baptist Journal of Theology* 15 (2011): 26.

5

Five 'Better-than' Statements

ECCLESIASTES 4

Qohelet leads us into the fray of the difficult task of negotiating life under the sun. His wisdom is dependable but provisional and relative. On the one hand, some things are better than others, especially companionship and moderate work. On the other hand, expecting too much from our labours (verses 7–8) or the people we lead (verses 13–16) is to be avoided.

It is important to hear Qohelet's 'better than' sayings in the context of his central teaching that there is 'nothing better than' enjoying life as a gift (2:24; 3:12–13). Qohelet is expanding the resources available to us as we negotiate life under the sun. While not allowing us to master existence, Qohelet still helps us live well.

Oppression, toil, friendlessness

4 Again I looked and saw all the oppression that was taking place under the sun:

I saw the tears of the oppressed –
    and they have no comforter;
power was on the side of their
    oppressors –
    and they have no comforter.
2 And I declared that the dead,
    who had already died,
are happier than the living,
    who are still alive.
3 But better than both
    is the one who has never
        been born,
who has not seen the evil
    that is done under the sun.

4 And I saw that all toil and all achievement spring from one person's envy of another. This too is meaningless, a chasing after the wind.

5 Fools fold their hands
> and ruin themselves.
6 Better one handful with
> tranquillity
> than two handfuls with toil
> and chasing after the wind.

7 Again I saw something meaningless under the sun:

8 there was a man all alone;
> he had neither son nor
> brother.
> There was no end to his toil,
> yet his eyes were not content
> with his wealth.
> 'For whom am I toiling,' he
> asked,
> 'and why am I depriving
> myself of enjoyment?'
> This too is meaningless –
> a miserable business!
9 Two are better than one,
> because they have a good
> return for their labour:
10 if either of them falls down,
> one can help the other up.
> But pity anyone who falls
> and has no one to help them
> up.
11 Also, if two lie down together,
> they will keep warm.
> But how can one keep warm
> alone?
12 Though one may be
> overpowered,
> two can defend themselves.
> A cord of three strands is not
> quickly broken.

Advancement is meaningless

13 Better a poor but wise youth than an old but foolish king who no longer knows how to heed a warning. **14** The youth may have come from prison to the kingship, or he may have been born in poverty within his kingdom. **15** I saw that all who lived and walked under the sun followed the youth, the king's successor. **16** There was no end to all the people who were before them. But those who came later were not pleased with the successor. This too is meaningless, a chasing after the wind.

1. Better the stillborn: oppression • Ecclesiastes 4:1–3

Coming on the heels of 3:16–22, this is another distressing passage. As I grow older, however, I am increasingly glad that I am not the only one who sometimes feels that the injustices of this life are so hideous, so unbearable, that they outweigh life itself. Non-existence might at times feel preferable to reading about or witnessing (much less living) those grievous abuses in which victims suffer not just helplessly, but alone (verse 1) – without any power to stand up or fight back, and even without any friend to sympathise. Anyone tempted to dismiss this as an overreaction is invited to do a little research on the worldwide industry of child sex trafficking, the way the kidnapped children are treated and the sickening amount of money it generates every year.

It is tempting to relieve one's horror at the violation of justice by loud calls for doing justice for the victimised. The Old Testament certainly makes such calls (e.g., Isaiah 1:16–17, 23), but Qohelet does not do so here. He sees, he mourns, but he does not call for any action. Sometimes nothing can be done. Recognising that sometimes we cannot even comfort victims, much less make their lives better (verse 1), is part of the painful wisdom of this part of God's word. 'What is crooked cannot be straightened' (1:15).

2. The absurdity of competitive jealousy • Ecclesiastes 4:4–6

Qohelet observes another *hebel*-absurdity: huge amounts of labour and skill (good things in themselves) are expended just to be better than someone else. The disproportion between the amount of excellent work and its motive is absurd. It forever amounts to chasing after the wind, because even if the one working successfully displaces their colleague, whatever fleeting satisfaction they get from their new position will not redeem all the work it took to get there.

But Qohelet is not recommending laziness (verse 5). Old

Testament wisdom literature is unanimous in the command to work hard (see, for example, Proverbs 6:6–11). Qohelet seconds this in the strongest possible way (he literally says, 'The fool folds his hands and eats his own flesh'). If our response to the endless and empty rat race is to do nothing, we are actually destroying ourselves. But between destructive laziness and useless overwork is a peaceful rest which, even when it works, disentangles itself from the dual futilities of jealous competition and of sloth (verse 6). Even if one has only a handful, that is better than an abundance of the alternatives.

3. The futility of overwork • Ecclesiastes 4:7–8

Qohelet provides a more involved example of verse 6. We can see what Qohelet really values in life under the sun in the way he diagnoses the uselessness of this man's life: endless work without family or heir, never enjoying the work as he was doing it, depriving himself of good meals with friends so he could log in more hours at the office – and to top it all off, never asking why he was bothering in the first place. Better at least to have had someone to pass an inheritance on to, or to have enjoyed the work itself, or to have leavened it with good vacations and meals (a 'handful with tranquillity', verse 6). Or at least he could have asked himself why he was bothering in the first place! None of these would have been perfect reasons for work, of course, for an heir might squander everything (2:19); and enjoying work or time off work is itself in vain because it is not enough in itself to redeem the hard hours of labour (2:1, 11). But any of these would have been better than such thoughtless wind-chasing.

FIVE 'BETTER-THAN' STATEMENTS

4. Don't be a loner • Ecclesiastes 4:9–12

Instead of the man working all alone (verse 8), companionship in work affords all kinds of opportunities for help, camaraderie and defence (verses 10–11). The 'return' of verse 9 is *śākār*, which often translates to payment for services rendered ('wages' in Genesis 30:28; see also Judges 9:4; 2 Samuel 10:6, among others). Working together promises a good return for that work.

There is no promise of escape from vanity here: a cord of three strands might not easily break, but it might break eventually. These are good things, but not absolute or inviolable goods. The wise embrace them without expecting too much or presuming that the screwiness of life under the sun (1:15) will never touch them.

5. The futility of wise leadership • Ecclesiastes 4:13–16

The Hebrew of these verses is difficult,[1] but the general point is clear: far better to enjoy a meteoric, rags-to-riches rise to success than to have all the power and privilege in the world and be so certain of yourself that you lose the ability to listen to anyone else. But, as elsewhere, this is no escape from vanity and absurdity: no matter how extensive the eventual reign of that poor wise youth, no one rejoiced in him in the end (verse 16). This, too, is *hebel*.

---

[1] The NIV makes a number of justified interpretative decisions in its translation, but various clauses could be taken in different ways. For example, it is possible that verse 14 describes the old king, not the youth (or that part of it does); and verse 15 might be talking about a third successor after the poor youth; see Fox, *A Time to Tear Down*, 224–7, for this reading. I am unsure how to resolve these questions, and commentators go different ways.

REFLECTION

Qohelet's wisdom is humble. His book is worlds away from the glittering but empty promises of a self-help guide; he does not claim to offer some magic key to a happy and untroubled life. I hope the modesty of Qohelet's 'better than' wisdom is not beneath any Christian when it may be exactly us who most need to reconsider why we are putting in such long hours at the office (verses 4–6), or why we are so intent on being a lone ranger (verse 9), or why we are so elated over the latest success story (verse 16). Perhaps we are irked more than we admit at the colleague who got a promotion we think should have gone to us (verse 4), and we work too hard as a result. Perhaps we are so certain of our own ideas (verse 13) that we endanger everything we labour for (verse 9). Recognising and accepting the limits God has placed on our lives will help us be at peace, even with a handful (verse 6).

6

True Piety

ECCLESIASTES 5:1–7

Acting as if your life is not subject to the brevity and futility of *hebel* can amount to failing to fear God. This will be evident in chattering, overconfident prayers and thoughtless vows. Recognising the distance between God and humanity will produce a quieter, calmer sort of spirituality which pleases God.

Fulfil your vow to God

5 [a] Guard your steps when you go to the house of God. Go near to listen rather than to offer the sacrifice of fools, who do not know that they do wrong.

2 Do not be quick with your mouth,
>do not be hasty in your heart
>to utter anything before God.
God is in heaven
>and you are on earth,
>so let your words be few.
3 A dream comes when there are
>many cares,
and many words mark the
>speech of a fool.

4 When you make a vow to God, do not delay to fulfil it. He has no pleasure in fools; fulfil your vow. **5** It is better not to make a vow than to make one and not fulfil it. **6** Do not let your mouth lead you into sin. And do not protest to the temple messenger, 'My vow was a mistake.' Why should God be angry at what you say and destroy the work of your hands? **7** Much dreaming and many words are meaningless. Therefore fear God.

---

[a] In Hebrew texts 5:1 is numbered 4:17, and 5:2-20 is numbered 5:1-19.

1. The right way to draw near to God • Ecclesiastes 5:1

The first imperative of the verse governs the whole passage: 'Guard your steps'. Although the verb (*šāmar*) is common in the Old Testament, a similar use is found in Deuteronomy, where God's people are repeatedly told to 'guard themselves', to keep a close watch on themselves, in covenant obedience (4:6, 15, 34; 6:12). The same connection between guarding yourself and obedience is found in our passage: in verse 1, the particular way you 'guard your steps' when you go to worship is by careful attention to everything God has to say ('Go near to listen'). In Hebrew, the word 'listen' (*šāmaʿ*) is the same as that for 'obey'. This is not a cautious, defensive listening which will decide later what it accepts or rejects; it is open, receptive and already ready to obey everything.

God values listening obedience far more than technically correct ritual and worship. 'The sacrifice of fools' means worship that outwardly conforms to God's standards but lacks heart-obedience. Qohelet is sounding a common biblical theme here: 'To obey is better than sacrifice' – even those sacrifices God commanded in the old covenant (1 Samuel 15:22; compare Romans 2:12–14). It does not even occur to some worshippers that going through the motions is not enough – a great folly, given the God before whom they stand.

Qohelet then spells out how we can guard ourselves in worship in two ways: thoughtless, incautious prayer and speech before God (verses 2–3) and vows (verses 4–7).

2. Guard your mouth • Ecclesiastes 5:2–3

There is a kind of hasty, overconfident speech before God which forgets the God we worship, which fails to guard itself (verse 1) in God's house. This verse is general enough to include prayer, as well as any sort of speech that happens during worship. 'God is in heaven and you are on earth' is an Old Testament way of expressing the infinite abyss which forever stands between Creator and creation. God is not one more factor in the world, however powerful; he exists forever above and independently of everything he has made. But it is possible to talk to and about God in a way that denigrates him to the level of a patron deity or business partner. NIV's 'cares' in verse 3 is better translated as 'business'; the same word is used in 1:13 for human activity in general. We can presumptuously talk in God's presence about everything we will accomplish, perhaps even intending to honour God as we do – but it is all a dream, and the talk of a fool who does not listen (verse 1). James 4:13–15 sounds almost the same note, exposing grandiose planning that ignores God – an especially arrogant thing for vanishing mist to do (a very 'Qoheletian' image).

Qohelet touches here on something very deep within us. There is something in the human heart that tends to denigrate God. It is as if we have a deep hankering for a god more like us; indeed, the gods of the great civilisations of the ancient Middle East were essentially humans writ large. This impulse to reduce God, to relate to him as if he were basically similar to us, is as dangerous as it is widespread.

The remedy to this is fewer words (verse 2). Perhaps creatures who had never fallen could engage in long prayers and many words without risking any presumptive unreality before the infinite, incomprehensible God they address. For those born under Adam and being redeemed in Christ, however, the best way to guard ourselves and honour God is to talk less.[1] 'In many words, sin is not lacking; but one who restrains his lips is wise' (Proverbs 10:19, author's translation).

---

[1] Jesus tells us not to babble in prayer as well, but for different reasons: to avoid ostentatious self-display and to avoid any sense of needing to get God's attention or remind him of our problems (Matthew 6:5–8).

3. Pay your vows • Ecclesiastes 5:4–7

A second way Qohelet helps us guard ourselves and honour God as God in worship has to do with following through on vows. Vows were common in the Old Testament in the form of a solemn promise of some gift or sacrifice made to God in the expectation of his intervention on behalf of the suppliant (see, for example, Genesis 28:20 Judges 11:30–31; 1 Samuel 1:11). A vow did not presume to force God to act, but was a concrete expression of faith that he would; it externalised the suppliant's faith by promising an offering to be given after God had acted. This is especially evident in the Psalms, when vows are paid to God in public worship, before the sight of all, to highlight God's faithful deliverance of the psalmist (Psalms 22:26; 50:14–15; 61:5, 8; 65:2; 66:13; 116:14, 18).

Qohelet's wisdom on vows is blunt: everything promised should be paid, and quickly (verse 4). Thoughtlessness will not be accepted as an excuse (verse 6).[2] Do not be caught up in religious excitement – if you are not sure whether you will be able to pay back your promise (or even want to), stay silent (verse 5; compare Proverbs 20:25). God will not bless the endeavours of those who make rash promises, benefit from God's action on their behalf and then fail to follow through ('destroy the work of your hands', verse 6). There exists an overconfident chatter which promises much but does not fear God (verse 7) and is deeply foolish (verse 4; the word 'fool' recurs in each section of this passage: verse 1, verse 3).

---

[2] The 'temple messenger' is a servant coming to collect what the suppliant promised. Qohelet simply uses the word 'messenger', however, which may refer to a human messenger or a divine one (the same word is frequently translated as 'angel' elsewhere in the Old Testament).

REFLECTION

Qohelet applies his main insight about brevity and vanity under the sun to worship, and especially to how we talk when we worship (he uses his favourite word, *hebel*, in verse 7). A failure to recognise and accept brevity and vanity which shows itself in presumptive and overconfident chattering can corrupt even sincere worship – worship that takes Scripture seriously and closely follows the New Testament's teaching on communion and baptism. The next time you go to church, listen to how those leading from the front talk – and to how you talk as well. Do we all speak as those standing before the Holy One, the 'I Am,' the one upon whom seraphim cannot bear to look (Isaiah 6:2)? Consider passages like Leviticus 9:23–4, where the fire of God's presence consumes the sacrifice and all the people shout and fall on their faces; or Revelation 1:12–18, where a saint no less than the apostle John cannot keep his feet before the resurrected Christ. If a non-Christian friend had to describe the kind of God you believe in based solely on how you talk about and to him, what would they say?

None of this is to deny the joy and comfort and welcome which every Christian receives every Sunday morning from God himself, or that boldness with which we can enter the holy places (Hebrews 10:19). But biblically speaking, joy and trembling never exclude each other; in fact, in the passage from Leviticus, the people 'shouted for joy' as they fell on their faces (the same verb is used repeatedly for joyful worship in the psalms, such as 95:1). Wise Christians, conscious that they are on earth and God is in heaven, will tremble as they rejoice and rejoice as they tremble (compare Psalm 2:11).

It is wise for us, living under the sun, who accomplish nothing of permanence during our short lives, to fear the one enthroned in the heavens (verse 7) by keeping strict guard on ourselves in worship (verse 1), with few words (verse 2) and assiduous completion on every pledge and promise (verse 4). There will be no shallowness, no sentimentality in how God is addressed. We will not pontificate about things we do not really understand, confident all the while that God is backing up everything we say; we will avoid pledging ourselves to different ministries or making great promises before God without cautiously counting the cost. God does not bless those who swagger and throw their weight around in church.[3]

---

[3] Eswine, *Recovering Eden*, 156. Eswine's discussion of this passage on pages 150–56 is excellent.

7

Wealth and Its Enjoyment

ECCLESIASTES 5:8–6:9

The happiness of wealth is deceptive and fragile. Enjoying your work now as your only portion from it, and eating and drinking as a gift from God, is much to be preferred to trying to find some settled happiness in wealth (5:18–20). The passage is structured chiastically (so the high point comes in the middle, not at the end) with two extended reflections on the vanity of trusting money (5:10–17, 6:1–9) surrounding a wiser approach to enjoying life (5:18–20).[1]

1. The unpredictability of wealth • Ecclesiastes 5:8–17

Riches are meaningless
8 If you see the poor oppressed in a district, and justice and rights denied, do not be surprised at such things; for one official is eyed by a higher one, and over them both are others higher still. **9** The increase from the land is taken by all; the king himself profits from the fields.

10 Whoever loves money never has enough;
whoever loves wealth is never satisfied with their income.
This too is meaningless.

11 As goods increase,
so do those who consume them.

---

[1] Taken, in a simplified form, from Seow, *Ecclesiastes*, 217.

And what benefit are they to the owners
    except to feast their eyes on them?

12 The sleep of a labourer is sweet,
    whether they eat little or much,
but as for the rich, their abundance
    permits them no sleep.

13 I have seen a grievous evil under the sun:

wealth hoarded to the harm of its owners,
14   or wealth lost through some misfortune,
so that when they have children there is nothing left for them to inherit.
15 Everyone comes naked from their mother's womb,
    and as everyone comes, so they depart.
They take nothing from their toil
    that they can carry in their hands.

16 This too is a grievous evil:

as everyone comes, so they depart,
    and what do they gain,
since they toil for the wind?
17 All their days they eat in darkness,
    with great frustration, affliction and anger.

This passage begins with two difficult verses. The first part of verse 8 is clear enough, but the reason why we should not be surprised at flagrant violations of justice could be read either positively or negatively: either one's outrage should be kept in check because higher officials will redress the wrongs of their subordinates, or we should not be surprised that a system of cronyism, where corrupt officials watch each other's backs, makes injustice inevitable. In my opinion, Qohelet's sensitivity to injustice makes the latter more likely. Regardless of which option one chooses, no call for reform is sounded (compare 4:1–3); violations of justice are inevitable, and it is naïve to be shocked when they happen.

Verse 9 is even more enigmatic, literally: 'The profit of a

land in every respect is this: the king is served by a field.'[2] Is the thought that an agrarian base is better than a self-serving bureaucracy? Or that the reliance of a society on agriculture prevents corruption from spreading too far? It is one of those rare verses where it is difficult to be certain, and I have yet to find any commentator who explains it satisfactorily.[3]

Fortunately, the rest of the passage is not so opaque. One of the vanities God imposes on life under the sun is that those who love money most enjoy it the least (verse 10; compare 1:8). The businessman John Rockefeller – who is generally considered to have been the wealthiest American of all time – was once asked how much money was enough. His reply? 'Just a little more.' There is a vanity, a futility, in building your bank account – the numbers will never be high enough to satisfy you. Besides, more money attracts more people who will want to leech it from you; you can enjoy looking at all your stuff, but it is all too easy for it to be sucked up by others, no matter how rich you get (verse 11). One reads sad stories of families torn apart by a single winning lottery ticket.

Another example of the strange twistedness of life under the sun comes in verse 12. While we would expect the rich man to be happy and his hired hands to be less so, the situation is often reversed: the latter work so hard that they sleep beautifully even if they eat meagrely, while the rich can barely close their eyes for fear of the stock market. Even stranger are those times when caution in business leads to bankruptcy and suffering for one's family (verses 13–17). Surely it is obvious that holding on to money until the right time is best for those who will inherit it?

---

[2] The Niphal of *'bd* is defined as 'be tilled' (*HALOT* 774; see Deuteronomy 21:4; Ezekiel 36:9, 34), but translating the verb this way in this verse produces nonsense: 'A king is tilled for a field.'

[3] See Seow, *Ecclesiastes*, 218–19; Fox, *A Time to Tear Down*, 234; Thomas Krueger, *Qoheleth*; trans. O. C. Dean (Minneapolis: Fortress, 2004), 113–15. Each provides extensive discussions, but none makes the verse 'click'.

But the crookedness of creation (1:15) means it is not always so. The anxiety and stressful toil of the work it took to accumulate that doomed fortune (verse 17) only makes the loss hurt more.[4]

2. Enjoy life as a gift from God • Ecclesiastes 5:18–20

18 This is what I have observed to be good: that it is appropriate for a person to eat, to drink and to find satisfaction in their toilsome labour under the sun during the few days of life God has given them – for this is their lot. **19** Moreover, when God gives someone wealth and possessions, and the ability to enjoy them, to accept their lot and be happy in their toil – this is a gift of God. **20** They seldom reflect on the days of their life, because God keeps them occupied with gladness of heart.

Qohelet returns to his central insight: in our brief and unpredictable lives, there is nothing better than to eat and drink and enjoy our work, for God has given these to us (verse 18). This is the central thread running through the book. It recalls much of the language used earlier to gain this insight: this is something Qohelet has seen (see 1:14; 2:24; 3:10, 16, 22; 4:1, 4, 7, 15; 5:13) about the simplest of pleasures (eating, drinking, work, as in 2:24, 3:12–13) during the number of our days (2:3), for our joy is our only portion, our only takeaway from our work, not any permanent profit (NIV's 'lot' in verse 18 is the same word as in 2:10, 3:22). This is more than a bland second-best; 'appropriate' in verse 18 is actually 'beautiful', recalling 3:11. Qohelet's enjoyment of even earthly gifts is enthusiastic: whether the meal is a full steak dinner or a salad, it is a gift from on high, and a beautiful one.

I mentioned above how the pleasures Qohelet recommends are

---

[4] The NIV's 'everyone' in verse 15 suggests a break in thought between verses 13–14 and 15–17, but the word is not present in the Hebrew; verses 13–17 describe and evaluate the same situation.

'democratic', available to everyone, regardless of social standing. This is certainly true for verse 18, but Qohelet gives an extra nuance in verse 19: if you are one of those few to whom God gives great wealth, along with the ability to enjoy it (see 6:2), then it should be enjoyed in the same way you would everything else – as a gift directly from God. (Among other blessings, this prevents any pride on the part of the wealthy. Money is God's gift, not something we infallibly earn for ourselves.)

In addition to receiving wealth as a gift, a curious secondary benefit attends the work that goes into making a pleasant life for yourself (verse 20). The 'days of their life' in Ecclesiastes has the connotation of whatever short amount of time God gives you (see 2:3; 5:17; 6:12; 8:15). We learn in verse 20 that God gives us enjoyable occupations which pleasantly absorb our attention, so that we do not think too much about our quickly approaching death. Qohelet will, of course, rigorously and uncomfortably focus our attention on death; in fact, he repeats the word 'remember' in 12:1 when speaking of our own funeral (see 12:5). But Qohelet understands that, however necessary it is sometimes to turn our attention to the grave, we cannot stay there. It is impossible to function if we think about nothing but death all the time. Our Creator understands our limitations. The heart of the wise is in the funeral home (7:1–4), but God also wisely gives us times of agreeably absorbing work to help us forget (5:20). There is a time for everything.

3. The unpredictability of wealth • Ecclesiastes 6:1–9

6 I have seen another evil under the sun, and it weighs heavily on mankind: **2** God gives some people wealth, possessions and honour, so that they lack nothing their hearts desire, but God does not grant them the ability to enjoy them, and strangers enjoy them instead. This is meaningless, a grievous evil.

³ A man may have a hundred children and live many years; yet no matter how long he lives, if he cannot enjoy his prosperity and does not receive proper burial, I say that a stillborn child is better off than he. ⁴ It comes without meaning, it departs in darkness, and in darkness its name is shrouded. ⁵ Though it never saw the sun or knew anything, it has more rest than does that man – ⁶ even if he lives a thousand years twice over but fails to enjoy his prosperity. Do not all go to the same place?

⁷ Everyone's toil is for their mouth,
    yet their appetite is never
    satisfied.
⁸ What advantage have the wise
    over fools?
What do the poor gain
    by knowing how to conduct
    themselves before others?
⁹ Better what the eye sees
    than the roving of the
    appetite.
This too is meaningless,
    a chasing after the wind.

Qohelet returns to the vanity of wealth, especially our inability to control it. Strange as it might seem, the possession of unlimited wealth does not guarantee its enjoyment; God can give one without the other (verses 1–2). Qohelet is greatly incensed by this, reserving some of his harshest rhetoric for it ('a grievous evil'). It is Qohelet's love of life as God's gift that makes him fulminate so: as far as he is concerned, it would be better to have been stillborn than to have had so much within your grasp, only to have the ability to enjoy it taken from you (verse 3). Qohelet explains his shocking reasoning in verses 4–6: both the frustrated rich and the stillborn end up in the same place eventually, but the stillborn is never vexed by the proximity of wealth which can never be enjoyed. Both wind up in the grave, but the rich has a much more unpleasant journey there. In that sense, the one at rest the whole time is to be preferred. Surprising as the passage is, it completely relativises all wealth in relation to the grave, and the wise take it to heart (compare 7:2).

Other asymmetries, other futilities, attend money and work in verses 7–9. All our work goes to feeding ourselves, but we only get hungry again (verse 7). This is as true for fools as it is for the wise – wisdom gives no advantage in this case (verse 8). Since it is gone so soon, it is better to enjoy what you can see now instead of hankering for what you used up yesterday or might enjoy tomorrow (the 'roving of the appetite', verse 9). But even this 'better' is an example of vanity, for it is absurd that we are often reduced to enjoying only what we see instead of actually possessing some good thing which we want but cannot get.

REFLECTION

This sometimes-shocking passage is of urgent relevance for every reader, regardless of socio-economic status. Qohelet does not rail against the rich, as some passages do (such as James 5:1–6); rather, the assumption is that wealth can be a good gift from God, to be enjoyed as such. Furthermore, Qohelet is aware that a lot of money can make life much easier (10:19). At the same time, Qohelet will not let us look away from the vanity of money, the ways in which its acquisition and enjoyment is subject to all kinds of futility and screwiness (1:15). Having it does not mean you will enjoy it (6:2); wise investments do not mean your children will (5:13–17). This is true for both rich and poor: the one who loves money, only to find out too late how unsatisfying it is (5:10), can be rich or poor.

Writing as an American, I can testify to the strange value we attribute to money which Qohelet's wisdom intends to unsettle. For Americans, a film or a company that makes more money is 'worth' more, literally and symbolically; we do not tend to view a lawyer struggling to make ends meet as equally successful to a rich one, even if they are equally skilled. It even bleeds in to how we talk: we 'value' relationships, we 'invest' time with others and so on.

But what strange defeats money inflicts on those who pursue it! Those who desire it most enjoy it least (5:10); it drives rest and refreshment from you (5:12); everything you worked so hard for can disappear in a single day (5:13, 17). The more there is, the more others will consume it (5:11). The wise take this to heart, surrender and enjoy each day as it comes from the hand of God, whether they are poor or rich (5:18).

8

What Is Really Good?

ECCLESIASTES 6:10–7:14

Qohelet reorients our instincts away from a superficial happiness which assumes a predictable and uninterrupted life and does not take account of God's imposition of frustration on creation (7:13). Using a prominent form of traditional wisdom ('better than'), he leads us in surprising and sobering directions, towards a sombre wisdom and a hard-won joy which fears God and accepts our ignorance and lack of control of the future.

1. Who can say what is good for man? • Ecclesiastes 6:10–12

¹⁰ Whatever exists has already been named,
    and what humanity is has been known;
no one can contend
    with someone who is stronger.
¹¹ The more the words,
    the less the meaning,
and how does that profit anyone?

¹² For who knows what is good for a person in life, during the few and meaningless days they pass through like a shadow? Who can tell them what will happen under the sun after they are gone?

God has imposed an order of repeating patterns on man (verse 10a, echoing 3:15 and 1:9). The patterns of human history and humanity itself are already known, predictable, unsurprising ('has already been named'); human beings have been doing the same kinds of things for millennia. This is another way of saying that there is nothing new under the sun. The one 'who is stronger' is God, who frustrates fallen creation in ways we cannot change (3:14). If we arrogantly presume that these patterns do not apply to us, or that we can win better lives for ourselves through our own ingenuity and industry (verse 10b), we attempt the impossible and only succeed in multiplying useless words that benefit no one (verse 11). Human beings cannot redesign reality according to our own specifications. This is another case where 'meaningless' as a translation for *hebel* is unfortunate, for the verse describes a lack of profit or benefit, not a lack of meaning. The situation Qohelet is describing is clear enough – it is one that it is useless to try to change.

Qohelet is still pursuing his central question about what is good for human beings, what is worth pursuing during our brief earthly lives (verse 12; see 2:3). Qohelet has already found some things that are good and has already passed on to us his insight that enjoyment of life as a gift is better by far than uselessly trying to establish some permanent significance for ourselves under the sun. But we have already seen how Qohelet's 'better than' wisdom implies its limitations: better, but not a perfect or an invulnerable good. These limitations occupy him more and more in chapters 7–9, especially our inability to predict the future (verse 12). If we knew what was coming down the line, we could be more certain about what is good to do now – but of course we don't. This means that the repeating patterns of history do not allow for predictions by which we could 'corner the market' and secure our existence and the results of our work. The crazy twists in life, the frustration God has imposed on creation, make this impossible (8:14; 9:2, 12). Much of the rest of this passage in 7:1–14 gives examples of people ignoring 6:10–12 and acting as if their lives will always be the same and that no future occurrence will disrupt their best-laid plans.

WHAT IS REALLY GOOD?

The way in which Qohelet sums up the major themes of chapters 1–3, evoking that vast image of generations ceaselessly rising and passing away, locked in the same patterns, signals a minor transition in the book. Qohelet is still pursuing what is good for a person in life (verse 12), but will now speak more about the unpredictability of the future. Despite the progress made, Qohelet still has much to teach us about fully recognising both the limitations and the goodness of life under the sun.

2. Death the teacher • Ecclesiastes 7:1–6

Wisdom

7 A good name is better than fine perfume,
    and the day of death better
        than the day of birth.
2 It is better to go to a house of
        mourning
    than to go to a house of
        feasting,
for death is the destiny of
    everyone;
    the living should take this to
        heart.
3 Frustration is better than
    laughter,
because a sad face is good for
    the heart.
4 The heart of the wise is in the
    house of mourning,
but the heart of fools is in the
    house of pleasure.
5 It is better to heed the rebuke of
    a wise person
than to listen to the song of
    fools.
6 Like the crackling of thorns
    under the pot,
so is the laughter of fools.
This too is meaningless.

Qohelet has already demonstrated his ability to shock the reader, but he outdoes himself in verse 1. Surely the birth of a new baby is in every way better than the loss of a human being in death? Part of the shock comes from the fact that Qohelet does not say why he thinks this, forcing us to stop and wonder how it could possibly be true (and, if you are like me, remaining mystified). Another part of the shock comes from the soothing effect of the first half of the verse, which raises expectations of something like Proverbs 22:1: 'A good name is more desirable than great riches; to be esteemed is better than silver or gold.' We should not, of course, skip by the first part of verse 1 too quickly: reputation is not everything, but it is a good thing, and we should be careful to guard closely the reputations of others in how we speak of them. But, of course, it is the second half of the verse that really interests Qohelet.

How is the day of death (mine or someone else's) better than the day of birth? Commentators usually turn to the way death delivers us from witnessing the miseries of life under the sun (4:1–3, 6:3), or (in relation to the first part of the verse) the fact that our reputation is not completely sealed and settled until one's life is over.[1] But neither of these is stated in this verse. Qohelet will later give us reasons why verse 1 is true, but for now he leaves us reeling, wondering what could possibly be preferable about death, and wondering what we have been missing all this time.

Once we start reading again, the picture comes into focus: the day of death is preferable because death is a better teacher than birth (verse 2). But unfortunately, not everyone listens. Fools fidget through a funeral, unable to do more than glance at the casket, and run to the pub as soon as the service is over; the wise stare at the coffin, accept that soon it will be their funeral which people will be attending, and ask themselves how they can live now so that they will not have regrets then (verse 2).[2] To use David's Gibson's striking expression, 'A coffin is a better preacher than a cot.'[3] Those who listen to the sermon and learn

---

[1] See, for example, Fox, *A Time to Tear Down*, 251–2.

[2] Gibson, *Destiny*, 88.

[3] Gibson, *Destiny*, 87. Please remember that Qohelet is addressing us in our earthly lives, helping us live wisely in the here and now, before the resurrection.

from it realise that 'the day of our coming death can be a friend to us in advance'.[4]

It was just this that Qohelet failed to do in chapter 2; the same failure to ask this question lies in the background of 4:8. Qohelet knows that many will refuse this lesson, staying at the party (the 'house of feasting' or 'house of pleasure' in verses 2, 4) and distracting themselves by taking turns at the karaoke machine (the 'song of fools' in verse 5). It is possible for Christians to do it as well. Worship can turn into a group exercise in self-distraction which leaves everyone feeling good and no one any wiser. (Take a moment to reflect on the last time a sermon confronted you with how soon you will be in the ground, or whether your church talks about death as much as the Bible does.)

In verse 3, we learn that Qohelet's wisdom is not nihilism or a perverse enjoyment of gloom for its own sake. It all leads to something good: there is a vexation, a frustration, which leads to a deeper and more stable joy (verse 3) than the laughter you hear at a party ('laughter' repeats in verses 3, 6). Putting verses 2–3 together shows us that, quite contrary to our natural intuitions about where happiness lies, facing the reality of death is a catalyst to joy in life now. You will never really value the next hour's work, the next meal, the next walk you take, until you deeply accept that soon your body will be a corpse, then a skeleton, then dust. It is a precious gift to have a joy in life which not even death can take from you, because you have already fully accounted for your own death. How much better Qohelet's wisdom than superficialities that are defenceless against the hard realities of life under the sun. The NIV's 'good for the heart' (verse 3) under-translates what is more literally 'the heart is good-ened' or 'the heart is made good;' a 'good heart' means enjoyment elsewhere in the book (9:7, 11:9). In its own way, this verse is as shocking as verse 1. Qohelet is showing us a joy

---

[4] Gibson, *Destiny*, 86.

in life which not even death can take away because death gives it to us. What a gift!

But the way verse 4 nuances verse 3 shows that this is a sombre joy. One does not attain the joy of truly attending to everything a funeral means and then leave grief behind forever. While fools run from sobering truths about a creation under frustration, the wise remain attentive, even if it spoils a certain kind of shallow happiness for them in the present.

One particular way in which wise men and women obey verse 4 is given in verses 5–6: they prefer even painful rebukes from wise people to laughing with people who will never challenge them. (How many wise Christian friends will tell you the absolute truth about yourself, no matter how it might sting?) The comparison to thorns in verse 6 suggests brevity and a hollowness (thorns burn quickly), as well as the irritation of self-distracting laughter (they make loud cracking noises when they burn). The Hebrew of verse 6 actually imitates the sound of burning thorns as well as the irritation of foolish laughter (*kî kĕqôl hasîrîm tahat hasîr kēn śĕhōq hakĕsîl*).

It is not immediately clear why Qohelet ends verse 6 with another statement of *hebel*/vanity, for none of the situations of verses 1–6 is exactly brief, nor is any of them obviously 'futile' or in vain or the like. Perhaps Qohelet ends the verse this way to lament the fact that laughter and partying would have such disappointing results (he wanted to enjoy these things in 2:1–8). Or perhaps he is generally shaking his head in bemused surprise at the strange way humans gain wisdom and joy.

WHAT IS REALLY GOOD?

3. Impatience, frustration, unpredictability
• Ecclesiastes 7:7–14

Wisdom
7 Extortion turns a wise person
   into a fool,
  and a bribe corrupts the
   heart.

8 The end of a matter is better
   than its beginning,
  and patience is better than
   pride.
9 Do not be quickly provoked in
   your spirit,
  for anger resides in the lap of
   fools.
10 Do not say, 'Why were the old
    days better than these?'
   For it is not wise to ask such
    questions.

11 Wisdom, like an inheritance, is a
    good thing
   and benefits those who see
    the sun.
12 Wisdom is a shelter
    as money is a shelter,
   but the advantage of knowledge
    is this:
   wisdom preserves those who
    have it.

13 Consider what God has done:

   who can straighten
    what he has made crooked?
14 When times are good, be happy;
    but when times are bad,
    consider this:
   God has made the one
    as well as the other.
   Therefore, no one can discover
    anything about their future.

Qohelet continues his counter-intuitive wisdom with a series of loosely related sayings about the realities of life under the sun for people who are not in control and cannot predict tomorrow.

First, although wisdom is an unambiguous good (2:13), it is not invulnerable. Having it does not guarantee you will never lose it (verse 7).[5] In light of this (as well as verses 1 and 3), verse

---
[5] Ellul, *Reason for Being*, 146.

8 is inescapable: the end of a thing is better than the beginning because we do not know how things will turn out (compare 6:12). For the same reason, patience is better than arrogantly assuming we already know the outcome – or can control it. We should take verse 8 in both a positive and a negative sense: a good beginning may be ruined (verse 7), and a depressing start may end in joy (verse 3). The limitations God has placed on human life call for patience if something does not instantly turn out well, instead of an arrogant certainty (8b) which explodes in anger when frustrated (verse 9).

A particular example of folly that is too-quickly vexed is romanticising the past (verse 10). This is unwise because it ignores the divinely imposed patterns on human history in 6:10 (since there is nothing new under the sun, whatever bothers you about the present existed back then too). It is also unwise because it ignores how a bad thing can turn out well (verse 8). Perhaps the evils of your day will be turned to immense good for your children.

In verses 11–12, we see that Qohelet's relentless attention to the limits of what we know is never meant to drive us to despair, or to imply that we know nothing at all about what is good under the sun (6:12), or that every choice is meaningless because nothing is better than anything else. Wisdom may be vulnerable (verse 7), externally unattractive (verse 2) and difficult to hear (verse 5), but it benefits the owner in very practical ways (verses 11–12). Your life will be preserved, enhanced and enriched in the same way that huge financial resources sweeten life and can also deliver from tragedies that would otherwise ruin you.

Qohelet closes this passage (verses 13–14) by recalling the picture of life under the sun presented in 6:10–12 (although not reflected in the NIV, the question in 7:13 is literally, 'Who is able to straighten?' echoing the same phrase in 6:10, 'No one is able to contend'). These closing two verses also confront us with our profound limitations under the sun. God's ordering of this age involves a kind of twisting which we cannot resolve (verse 13). The language of crookedness is different, but this is surely close to Qohelet's main thesis about *hebel*: there is a screwiness, an unpredictability, to life under the sun; we cannot hold it within our grasp or guarantee results or even anticipate what is coming. All we can do is receive and respond to what comes; enjoy good days and take to heart the lesson of bad ones. We have absolutely no idea what the future holds (verse 14).

David Gibson puts it this way:

> Stop thinking the future will be better and easier. Stop thinking that if only things were different you would be a better person . . . You do not know the future . . . Perhaps these are indeed the very best days of my life. Maybe I'll be dead tomorrow. Live the life you have now instead of longing for the life you think you will have, but which you actually cannot control at all.[6]

REFLECTION

As a boy, I lived in Banchory, Scotland, while my father studied at Aberdeen. We attended the local west side kirk and our family somehow managed to inherit a number of the church's hymnals – small blue books first published in 1898. I took one when I left for college. Perusing it, I am always struck by the number of bad hymns sung by our forebears that are best left behind, as well as the many gems that are presently neglected or forgotten. Just as striking is the way almost all of the good ones talk about death: 'O Sacred Head Now Wounded' asks, 'Be near me, Lord, when dying/O show thy cross to me.'[7] 'Whate'er my

---

[6] Gibson, *Destiny*, 63.
[7] Paul Gerhardt (1607–76), translated by James W. Alexander (1844–1930), 'O Sacred Head Now Wounded'. Public domain.

God Ordains is Right' has the promise, 'Though sorrow, need, or death be mine/Yet I am not forsaken.'[8] 'Guide me, O Thou Great Jehovah' ends with: 'When I tread the verge of Jordan/Bid my anxious fears subside.'[9] And who can forget the drawing of that fleeting breath and eyelids closing in death which ends 'Rock of Ages'?[10] The generations who passed their faith on to us were singing about death all the time. The hymnal even has a separate section for funerals.

Reading Ecclesiastes 6:10–7:14 and reflecting on my own experience of years of worship in modern Western evangelical settings, I cannot help but feel that it counts as a written rebuke from a wise friend (7:5) which stings because it hits the mark. My experience may not be representative, and I am anxious to avoid any hint of ingratitude to the preachers and worship leaders who sacrificially passed on their faith to me. At the same time, I cannot avoid the sense that we are better at entertaining and creating good feelings in worship than growing in the kind of wisdom Qohelet describes. Huge amounts of talent, money and practice are put into modern worship, but do guitar solos confront me with my profound inability to control my life, or even predict where it will go? Are church building projects explicitly undertaken in light of passages like Ecclesiastes 7:13–14? How often am I made uncomfortable in church with truths I know but would rather avoid about my mortality? The conversations, the tone from up front, the 'feel' of the music: how much of it is meant to comfort in ways Qohelet would find superficial? Do our churches resemble the 'house of feasting' or the 'house of pleasure' (7:2, 4) more than we realise?

---

[8] Samuel Rodigast (1649–1708), translated by Catherine Winkworth (1804–59), 'Whate'er My God Ordains Is Right'. Public domain.
[9] William Williams (1717–91), translated by Peter Williams (1723–96), 'Guide Me O Thou Great Redeemer'. Public domain.
[10] Augustus Toplady (1740–78), 'Rock of Ages'. Public domain.

WHAT IS REALLY GOOD?

Ecclesiastes 7 is not the only chapter in the Bible, and the psalms are full of both joyful hymns and laments. At the same time, perhaps I should not be so flummoxed when Qohelet tells me that the day of death is better than the day of birth. Perhaps the verse is not really so shocking after all. Perhaps it only shocks those (like me) untrained in the sort of wisdom Qohelet passes on – wisdom that comes ultimately from God (12:11). Let none of us refuse this gift: through this book, God is giving the only kind of joy not easily punctured by the realities of brevity and vanity in life under the sun.

9

Righteousness and Wisdom Subject to Vanity

ECCLESIASTES 7:15–29

Righteousness and wisdom, necessary and beneficial as they are, are subject to vanity. Your life will not automatically be better if you are good, and no comprehensively coherent worldview, no satisfying closure, will be yours if you are wise.

1. *The futility of being righteous • Ecclesiastes 7:15–18)*

15 In this meaningless life of mine I have seen both of these:

the righteous perishing in their righteousness,
and the wicked living long in their wickedness.
16 Do not be over-righteous, neither be overwise – why destroy yourself?
17 Do not be overwicked, and do not be a fool – why die before your time?
18 It is good to grasp the one and not let go of the other. Whoever fears God will avoid all extremes.[a]

---
a 18 Or *will follow them both*

A quick word on a central theme of Old Testament wisdom literature will help this short passage come into appropriately sharp relief. The backbone of books like Proverbs is that God has ordered his creation such that humble obedience brings great blessing, while ignoring God and putting yourself first destroys the fool.[1] The way biblical sages point to patterns in creation does not remove God from the picture: Proverbs and Psalms continually show God upholding the moral order of his world and directly intervening for his saints and against rebels. There is, however, a profound sense in which everyone also reaps what they sow. We see both sides in Psalm 7:11–16, where God both directly judges the wicked (verses 12–13), but also lets their own violence return on their head (verses 15–16).

Within these divinely ordained patterns, 'long life' is shorthand for the blessings that accrue to faithful obedience (Proverbs 3:2; compare Psalm 34:12–14). Length implies quality; Proverbs labours to convince us that the fear of the Lord will make the greatest of differences in the here and now. In his generosity, our Lord promises us not only eternal life, but also joy in our earthly lives to those who trust and follow him. This means that when Qohelet describes the wicked 'living long in their wickedness' in verse 15, he is evoking this central wisdom tenet and admitting that he has empirical evidence ('I have seen') that it is not always true – not in obvious ways, at least. Worsening things is that Qohelet sees this as an ongoing problem, not an occasional exception: the verse could be translated such that Qohelet saw how the wicked 'kept on living long in their wickedness'.[2]

I hope we appreciate Qohelet's dilemma. Isn't it intuitively obvious that people who fear, trust and follow God will flourish in the world he created, while those who ignore him and live according to their own ideas will only damage themselves? At the same time, surely every reader can think of flagrantly selfish

---

[1] Bruce Waltke writes, 'The righteous . . . are willing to disadvantage themselves to advantage the community; the wicked are willing to disadvantage the community to advantage themselves.' Bruce Waltke, *The Book of Proverbs: Chapters 1–15* (Grand Rapids: Eerdmans, 2004), 97.

[2] The participles in this verse can express an ongoing state of affairs or continuous/repeated action (WOC 37.6d). This implies that Qohelet has witnessed the 'blessings of sin' more than once.

RIGHTEOUSNESS AND WISDOM SUBJECT TO VANITY

people who seem to win for themselves that long life, wealth and honour promised to the wise (Proverbs 3:1–10). How can this be? Qohelet himself seems surprised at what he sees. The beginning of the verse should be translated not 'both' but 'everything';[3] we can imagine Qohelet shaking his head as he admits: 'I've seen everything in my crazy life!'[4]

Qohelet's takeaway from this distressing reality is fascinating and, I believe, unparalleled in the Old Testament. He draws two conclusions from verse 15 in verses 16–17. First, he tells us not to be 'over-righteous' or excessively wise (verse 16).[5] Since righteousness is never elsewhere prescribed a limit in the Old Testament, this is a surprising thing to say, but the final question in the verse explains Qohelet's caution. The verb at the end of the verse can mean 'to be destroyed', but the particular form used elsewhere means 'to be appalled' or 'to be struck dumb with horror'.[6] So what kind of super-righteousness might be shocked beyond all measure (verse 16) when it witnesses wickedness reaping blessing and righteousness being destroyed (verse 15)? An obvious candidate would be a kind of spirituality that has not fully reckoned with the reality of *hebel* and the twistedness God has imposed on creation – the way in which the race does not always belong to the swift (9:11) and expected results are not always obtained. This kind of spirituality exerts itself tirelessly on God's behalf, which is good. But it also promises itself great blessing for its labours with complete certainty. When this kind of spirituality finally cannot

---

[3] 'Both' would be *šĕnêhem*, 'the two of them'; Qohelet writes *kōl*, 'all' or 'every'.
[4] This is not to say that Ecclesiastes contradicts Proverbs; see Introduction.
[5] The Hitpael form of 'be wise' can be translated as 'pretend to be wise', i.e., to put on airs that you are wiser than you really are (GKC 54.3). But since the wicked in the next verse are not pretending to be wicked, it is best to take it as a reflexive, 'make yourself excessively wise'.
[6] See *HALOT* 1566; normally the Qal expresses destruction, with the Hitpael (used in verse 15) expressing shock. *HALOT* combines both senses in reference to this verse, translating as 'bring oneself to ruin'.

deny any longer the reality that sometimes the most godly lives are the most miserable, it is shocked, offended, horrified and in danger of giving up on God altogether and destroying itself. This is a righteousness brittle in its naïveté. As we will see in verse 18, it is possible to pursue righteousness in a way that does not fear God.

Should obeying God be abandoned, then? We can hear echoes of Paul's 'By no means!' from Romans 6:2 in verse 17. Wickedness and folly are to be avoided just as much as the gullible spirituality of verse 15, with the same high stakes: 'Why die before your time?' (verse 17). Qohelet speaks of being 'overwicked' in this verse, not to imply that a little sin can be indulged with impunity but to warn against an attitude that throws itself into sin when it sees the apparent lack of consequences in verse 15. Qohelet warns (along with the rest of Scripture) that the wages of sin is death (compare Romans 6:23), and those practising it unrepentantly destroy themselves. Dying 'before your time' means an unfortunately early death – that is, one that misses the 'long life' of blessing so often promised to those who fear God in Proverbs and Psalms. In other words, dying 'before your time' alludes to that great wisdom theme of people reaping what they sow (see the same in Job 22:16). I hope the reader sees the obvious 'contradiction' here. In verse 15, the wicked are living unexpectedly long, happy lives; in verse 17, they die early, as expected. So which is it?

Qohelet does not choose and does not ask us to. He does not conclude from the distressing reality of verse 15 that nothing matters and one might as well disobey God. He accepts, along with the rest of Old Testament wisdom, that God is at work in all things and that obedience rewards itself in practical and immediate ways, while rebellion against God destroys itself (verse 17). He also freely admits those exceptions where the opposite seems to be the case (verse 15). He does not allow these exceptions to destroy his faith, but neither does he let his faith blind him to the exceptions (we will see this again in 8:12–14). He holds on to God's promises while remaining utterly realistic about the world. We have probably all

RIGHTEOUSNESS AND WISDOM SUBJECT TO VANITY

heard of or known people who seemed interested in Christianity, only to abandon it as soon as they discovered even small problems or apparent contradictions. Qohelet's flexibility is wiser.

To 'grasp the one' and 'not let go of the other' in verse 18 means attending to and remembering the equal danger of naïve super-righteousness and wickedness. Qohelet studied both, seeking to understand wisdom and folly without engaging in the latter (1:17; 7:25), and urges us to do the same. The NIV's 'avoid all extremes' makes sense because of the language of 'over-righteous' and 'overwicked' in verses 16–17, but mistranslates the Hebrew, which literally says 'the one fearing God will go forth from them all'.[7] The same verb is used in 1 Samuel 14:41 meaning 'to escape', which seems to be the sense here – an appropriate fear of God will help you escape from both brittle super-righteousness and immersion in wickedness. That same pious and reverent fear of God that restrains overconfident verbosity in God's presence (5:2–3) also recognises the futility he has imposed on creation and accepts that obedience may not always pay off exactly or immediately in the ways we expect. As elsewhere in his book, Qohelet is thinking through the implications of *hebel* (futility and disproportion) in relation to different subjects – here, spirituality and obedience.

I hope, at this point, the unique pastoral importance of this passage is clear. God, in his generosity, rewards faithful saints both in the life of the world to come and in their earthly lives. However, if these rewards always came quickly, obviously and

---

[7] The NIV may also be influenced by a theory that Hellenistic ideals of moderation and the golden mean in ethics stand behind this passage. See further the interpretations summarised by Wayne Brindle, 'Righteousness and Wickedness in Ecclesiastes 7:15–18', in *Reflecting with Solomon: Selected Studies on the Book of Ecclesiastes*, ed. Roy Zuck (Grand Rapids: Baker, 1994), 302–4. I believe Ecclesiastes predates the Hellenistic period, however; and in any case, it is not what the Hebrew says. The NIV footnote that suggests 'follow them both' is also a mistranslation; the normal expression for 'following' in Hebrew is (among other possibilities) 'to walk after' (as in, for example, 1 Kings 18:21).

automatically, it would be easy to take a 'slot machine' approach to God; faith would be displaced by an automatic process of earning rewards for good behaviour. God allows temporary exceptions and delays to saints reaping what they sow in order to purge faith of any ulterior motive. Real saints maintain loyalty with God even when it does not quickly benefit them, trusting God to let them reap what they sow in his time and way.

2. *The real but limited value of wisdom* • *Ecclesiastes 7:19–22*

19 Wisdom makes one wise person
    more powerful
      than ten rulers in a city.

20 Indeed, there is no one on earth
    who is righteous,
      no one who does what is
        right and never sins.

21 Do not pay attention to every
    word people say,
      or you may hear your servant
        cursing you –

22 for you know in your heart
    that many times you yourself
      have cursed others.

Qohelet will elsewhere engage in short, self-contained proverbs which move quickly from one subject to another. Each one of his proverbs is worth considering in its own right; but a little reflection will also suggest ways that each can be read in a sequence, such that each comments on and nuances the others. This is the case in 7:19–22, where Qohelet begins by nuancing his exploration of the limits of what righteousness and wisdom can expect in this life (verses 15–18) with a statement of what impressive results wisdom can achieve: it gives more strength to one wise person than ten powerful rulers with huge resources ('in the city').

    The next verse does not rescind the great potential of wisdom, but does temper it: no matter how you grow in righteousness, sin will always dog you and limit your effectiveness (verse 20;

RIGHTEOUSNESS AND WISDOM SUBJECT TO VANITY

as in verses 15, righteousness and wisdom, though distinct, are always joined).[8] A particular example of verse 20 is given in verses 21–22, with a moral drawn: it is inappropriate to blow up at criticism when you are guilty of the same.

3. Wise reflection on wisdom • Ecclesiastes 7:23–9

23 All this I tested by wisdom and I said,

> 'I am determined to be wise' –
>   but this was beyond me.
> 24 Whatever exists is far off and
>   most profound –
>   who can discover it?
> 25 So I turned my mind to
>   understand,
>   to investigate and to search
>   out wisdom and the
>   scheme of things
> and to understand the stupidity
>   of wickedness
> and the madness of folly.
>
> 26 I find more bitter than death
>   the woman who is a snare,
> whose heart is a trap
>   and whose hands are chains.
> The man who pleases God will
>   escape her,
>   but the sinner she will
>   ensnare.
> 27 'Look,' says the Teacher,[b] 'this is what I have discovered:
>
> 'Adding one thing to another to
>   discover the scheme of
>   things –
> 28 while I was still searching
>   but not finding –
> I found one upright man among
>   a thousand,
>   but not one upright woman
>   among them all.
> 29 This only have I found:
>   God created mankind upright,
>   but they have gone in search
>   of many schemes.'

---

b 27 Or *the leader of the assembly*

---

[8] That is to say, you cannot be insightful about the complex ordering of God's world without being moral, nor a moral person without wise insight into the complications of life. It is significant in this connection that Proverbs will refer to and recommend 'righteousness' and 'wisdom' almost the same number of times; see Eric Ortlund, 'The Pastoral Implications of Wise and Foolish Speech in the Book of Proverbs', *Themelios* 38 (2013): 7, note 1.

We mentioned above how Qohelet does more than analyse and interpret life under the sun; he analyses his own analyses, reflecting on his own thinking and drawing further conclusions (see 1:16–18). A curious and admirable mixture of conviction and humility follows. We see this first in verses 23–4, where Qohelet pulls back and relates how he tested 'all this' by wisdom, referring to his conclusions earlier in the chapter. This means, on the one hand, that wisdom was available to Qohelet, providing the means by which he reaches the conclusions of verses 1–22. At the same time, wisdom escapes him (verse 23): he knows some things, but (as we will see below) any kind of comprehensive or perfect resolution to life's questions eludes him. As in 7:15–18, Qohelet joins together what we might tend to separate. The limitations of his wisdom do not drive him to scepticism, but he does not overrate himself on the basis of the few things he does know.

In verse 24, 'whatever exists' is better taken as 'what has been';[9] if Qohelet had better knowledge of the past – the repeating patterns of which continue into the present – he would not be so limited in making sense of life now. But it is too deep for him to plumb. Anyone who reads any history will know that piecing together the different causes of historical events of even a few centuries ago can be very difficult, much less the distant past.

Qohelet's meagre wisdom is not owing to lack of effort on his part, however. He describes at length in verse 25 his painstaking search to understand life under the sun (recalling 1:13, 17; 2:12). He then lists the results of his lifetime of labour in verses 26–9. These results are decidedly mixed. Using the word 'find' seven times, Qohelet is able to gain certainty about a few things, but

---

[9] The same Hebrew phrase identifies what has happened in the past as opposed to the present in 1:9; 3:15; 6:10. Old Testament wisdom is especially oriented towards the past, as well as receiving wisdom from elders (see, for example, Job 15:7–10).

RIGHTEOUSNESS AND WISDOM SUBJECT TO VANITY

he fails to find some overall rationale or comprehensive perspective or satisfying closure (the 'scheme of things' in verse 25).[10]

First, Qohelet finds how dangerous and bitter the adulterous woman is – a woman who uses her sexuality only to entrap, outside any intention of love and commitment (verse 26).[11] This is an urgent and important lesson for anyone growing in wisdom to learn, but it is hardly a surprise; Proverbs 5–7 expound on the danger of this sort of person at length. Second, he found a single faithful friend out of a thousand (not very good odds), but not a single faithful woman (verses 27–8). This is not a misogynistic dismissal of all women, as if women are worse than men, because Qohelet consigns both genders equally under sin in verse 29, and also blesses marriage in 9:9. The fact that Qohelet could not find a faithful woman does not mean she does not exist, only that women (and men) of such quality are rare (compare Proverbs 18:22). But the one thing Qohelet did find ('this only') is that human beings violate their Creator's righteous and morally beautiful design for them and engage in all kinds of scheming (verse 29).

I cannot avoid a sense of anticlimax here. All that intellectual labour (verse 25), just to discover that some women are dangerous, friends are hard to come by and people are sinners. Qohelet himself seems dissatisfied with the result when he refers to what his soul sought and did not find in verse 28. He wanted more. But Qohelet is forthright about the humble results of his lifelong search. This, too, is part of wisdom.

---

[10] The word translated 'scheme' occurs only elsewhere in the Old Testament in verses 27, 29, and 2 Chronicles 26:15, where it refers to war machines. The paucity of usage makes it difficult to define the word precisely, but the 'schemes' of verse 29 are clearly sinful plans, while the use in verse 27, where Qohelet adds 'one thing to another', suggests some more comprehensive account of the nature of life under the sun. NIV's 'scheme of things' communicates this well.
[11] Eswine, *Recovering Eden*, 181–2.

REFLECTION

I remember a fascinating conversation with a Christian friend who confessed to struggling with anger towards God for some time. He had been pursuing a young woman, but when the romance soured, the normal hurt feelings and disappointment were sharpened by a resentment towards God. My friend told me it took him a while to realise the source of his anger: he had made an unconscious assumption that sticking close to God and taking discipleship seriously (he was a pious young man) would mean that his life would work out in expected ways and he wouldn't get hurt. As soon as he realised he had made this assumption, he realised how laughable it was; without meaning to, he had strayed into the dangerous territory of naïve righteousness which can be shattered by the hard realities of living after the fall (7:15–18). His mistake is an understandable and common one. It is easy to promise yourself too much from life under the sun because you are (or think you are) a good Christian.

Just as common is the presumption that thinking hard, reading lots and growing in wisdom will deliver to you some perfect world view which will give you satisfying closure on life's mysteries. I laboured for much of my twenties under this illusion; as a teacher in a theological college, I can attest I am not the only one who falls into this trap. 'I tested everything by wisdom – I said, 'I will be wise' – but it is far from me' (verse 23, my translation). Is any of us in a different position? This is a long way away from total scepticism, but it is a deeply humble wisdom that is entirely unpretentious about its severe limitations. You could have an IQ of 150, a vast library and near limitless energy to read, and life would still be mysterious, except for a few bedrock certainties like the universality of sin. Nothing less than God's word itself brings us back down to earth so emphatically. The wise accept it, along with every other limitation God places on us.

10

Acting Wisely Before the King

ECCLESIASTES 8:1–9

Qohelet guides those in leadership under the king in light of the under-the-sun realities of unpredictability and vanity (verse 7). Despite the precariousness of this kind of position, and despite the difficulties of life under the sun, right action and success are still possible.

8 Who is like the wise?
　Who knows the explanation of
　　things?
A person's wisdom brightens
　　their face
and changes its hard appearance.

Obey the king
2 Obey the king's command, I say, because you took an oath before God. **3** Do not be in a hurry to leave the king's presence. Do not stand up for a bad cause, for he will do whatever he pleases. **4** Since a king's word is supreme, who can say to him, 'What are you doing?'

5 Whoever obeys his command
　　will come to no harm,
and the wise heart will know
　　the proper time and
　　procedure.
6 For there is a proper time and
　　procedure for every matter,
though a person may be
　　weighed down by misery.

7 Since no one knows the future,
　　who can tell someone else
　　what is to come?
8 As no one has power over the
　　wind to contain it,
so[a] no one has power over
　　the time of their death.
As no one is discharged in time
　　of war,
　so wickedness will not release
　　those who practise it.

9 All this I saw, as I applied my mind to everything done under the sun. There is a time when a man lords it over others to his own[b] hurt.

a 8 Or *over the human spirit to retain it, / and so*
b 9 Or *to their*

1. *The value of wisdom* • *Ecclesiastes 8:1*

The 'explanation of things' is literally 'the interpretation of a thing'. This calls to mind Joseph (Genesis 41) and Daniel (Daniel 2), whose interpretations of dreams were of dire importance to kingdoms when the kings themselves were flummoxed and helpless.[1] The rhetorical question opening the verse suggests the incomparable value of those who can understand, interpret, negotiate and resolve those otherwise impossible problems that can destroy nations (compare Isaiah 19:11–15, where the failure of royal council spells doom for Egypt, powerful as it is). Such wisdom is a source of relief and joy ('brightens their face') for everyone, but most of all for the wise man or woman who speaks it. 'Hard appearance' is literally 'strength of face', which means a harsh and ruthless attitude (Deuteronomy 28:50; Daniel 8:23). Wisdom and understanding are happier and more effective than affecting a brazen confidence or trying to master problems by strength alone.

2. *Submission to royal sovereignty* • *Ecclesiastes 8:2–4*

The fact that the wise man or woman might better understand how to negotiate some issue does not mean they should put

---

[1] To whatever extent Joseph and Daniel are good parallels, it is worth noting that both give credit for interpretation to God alone (Genesis 41:16; Daniel 2:27–8). This, too, is part of wisdom.

on airs or forget their station. The wise submit to the king, avoiding any attempt to undermine the king's authority ('stand up for a bad cause' is literally 'stand in an evil matter'). In fact, they avoid even the appearance of doing so (i.e., by hurrying 'to leave the king's presence' in some shifty way). Verse 4 gives one reason why, suggesting not just the king's unlimited ability to punish, but also his authority in a more general sense: it is not a royal counsellor's place to second-guess their sovereign or call him to account. Daniel is an excellent example of this. Finding himself in the unenviable position of serving the very king who exiled his own people, he nevertheless works for the benefit of Nebuchadnezzar and his rule (Daniel 4:19) while also clearly calling him to repent (verse 27). Christians need not choose between craven capitulation and sedition.

The 'oath before God' in verse 2 is a possible interpretation of what is literally 'the oath of God'; this could be an oath made to God or one made by God to the king. My sense is that the latter is better because of other passages that show divine authority standing behind human authority, whether Israelite (Psalm 110:4) or Gentile (Romans 13:1). This provides an even stronger reason to obey (verse 2).

3. The right time to act • Ecclesiastes 8:5–8

Qohelet combines the blessed potential of wisdom from verse 1 and the importance of obedience from verse 2 with his larger theme of the limitations of wisdom owing to our ignorance of the future.

In verse 5, the one (literally) 'guarding the command' (i.e., obeying verse 2) knows the right time and appropriate way forward in every situation (verse 1), however diverse or difficult they might be. The 'command' of this verse could be the king's or God's; since God legitimates human authority, the ambiguity may be deliberate. NIV's 'will come to no harm' translates 'knows no evil thing'; in the light of the similar phrases in the second half of the verse and in verse 1, this probably complements the wise person 'guarding the command' in the sense of not getting involved in any plot against the king. Qohelet's wisdom is one of unambiguous submission to authority, mixed with dogged and optimistic persistence in dealing with problems (even if the king is part of the problem). We see this especially in verse 6, where wisdom can find solutions to problems even in the worst of situations (verse 6, literally, when 'the evil [or misfortune] of man lies heavy upon him').[2]

In verses 7–8, Qohelet continues to steer between scepticism and presumption. While wisdom is of benefit even in very unfortunate circumstances (verse 6), it is forever bounded by our ignorance and lack of control. We cannot predict how things will go in a general sense (verse 7), while the one certainty we have of death is as far outside of our control as the wind (8a). In other words, there is so much we do not know, and the one thing we do know is entirely out of our control. Furthermore, there are times when we will find ourselves very likely to die, without possibility of escape (8b). None of these limitations, however, means that there is any refuge in sin (8b), which will

---

[2] NIV's 'proper time and procedure' translates 'time and justice'. The phrase is probably a hendiadys, i.e., a single idea expressed by two words, just as 'righteousness and justice' in the Old Testament often means 'righteous judgment'. Interpreting this as 'the appropriate time for the right decision' is entirely plausible, but since *mišpaṭ* can mean 'judgment' either in the sense of a human decision or in the sense of divine judgment, it is equally possible to read verses 5–6 as saying that the wise person does not get involved in anything inappropriate (know 'any evil thing') because they know God's judgment is coming soon (verse 5) – every matter will receive judgment, because humanity's evil lies heavily upon them (verse 6). Qohelet's phrasing makes either reading plausible; in the interface of human and divine wisdom in the sphere of government, it could be that both are meant.

destroy those who give themselves to it as surely as would a charging army.

Wisdom might make a man's face shine, but wisdom cannot insulate you against the repeating patterns God imposes on life under the sun.

4. Qohelet's final reflection • Ecclesiastes 8:9

Qohelet's guidance in this passage comes from his thorough examination of the vicissitudes of royal life, even in the worst of circumstances, when a king rules to the hurt of others. Qohelet's call to submit is not made because of some naïve idealisation of life in the court; but by the same token, the possibility of wise interpretation (verse 1) and the right time to act (verse 5) are not cancelled by an unwise king who harms those under his rule.

REFLECTION

For Christians working in government (or other positions of high influence and authority), this passage is both hopeful and sobering. God himself can be at work through you to resolve deeply complex and seemingly intractable problems in ways that can benefit myriads of others (verses 1, 5); but even these best possibilities are bounded by human limitation and lack of control (verses 7–8). Your role is to stay at your post (verses 2–3), working for the public good, even if those in authority over you fail those they claim to serve (verse 9).

11

The Problem of Delayed Judgment

ECCLESIASTES 8:10–17

Without surrendering his faith, Qohelet admits that God's ordering and governance of the world is beyond our comprehension, especially with regard to the treatment of those faithful to God and those rebelling against him. In light of this, there is nothing better than to enjoy the gifts God gives us now.

¹⁰ Then too, I saw the wicked buried – those who used to come and go from the holy place and receive praise[c] in the city where they did this. This too is meaningless.

¹¹ When the sentence for a crime is not quickly carried out, people's hearts are filled with schemes to do wrong. ¹² Although a wicked person who commits a hundred crimes may live a long time, I know that it will go better with those who fear God, who are reverent before him. ¹³ Yet because the wicked do not fear God, it will not go well with them, and their days will not lengthen like a shadow.

¹⁴ There is something else meaningless that occurs on earth: the righteous who get what the wicked deserve, and the wicked who get what the righteous deserve. This too, I say, is meaningless. ¹⁵ So I commend the enjoyment of life, because there is nothing better for a person under the sun than to eat and drink and be glad. Then joy will accompany them in their toil all the days of the life God has given them under the sun.

¹⁶ When I applied my mind to know wisdom and to observe the labour that is done on earth – people getting no sleep day or night – ¹⁷ then I saw all that God has done. No one can comprehend what goes on under the

sun. Despite all their efforts to search it out, no one can discover its meaning. Even if the wise claim they know, they cannot really comprehend it.

c 10 Some Hebrew manuscripts and Septuagint (Aquila); most Hebrew manuscripts *and are forgotten*

1. Qohelet's realism and faith • Ecclesiastes 8:10–13

Verse 10 is difficult to translate,[1] but clearly Qohelet is grieved by the praise that the worst sorts of people receive when the opposite should be the case. This is not meaningless, but absurd (see comment on 1:2); it is not a situation without any meaning, but has a meaning contrary to all reasonable expectation. Worse yet, the happy lives of people living in open rebellion towards God emboldens others to sin recklessly (verse 11).

Qohelet does not minimise or ignore these apparent exceptions to the reality of God's justice and judgment. At the same time, he will not allow them to shake his conviction ('I know') that committing to the fear of the Lord – whatever sacrifice this entails – is in every way better (verse 12). It does not matter how apparently successful and flourishing a wicked life is, or what you have to give up to maintain loyalty to God; it will be better for you in the end, and flagrant rebellion against God will be exposed and judged (verse 13).

---

[1] The Hebrew seems to have suffered damage in transmission, literally reading, 'Then I saw the wicked buried, and they went, and from the holy place they walk about, and they were forgotten in the city where they did thus.' Two slight emendations on the basis of the Greek Septuagint yield the more coherent: 'Then I saw the wicked brought to their graves; and from the holy place they walk about and they are praised in the city, where they acted thus,' i.e., those burying the dead go forth from the Temple grounds and continue to praise them in the very place they acted wickedly. If this is correct, it depicts a situation worse than the rendering of the NIV, for these wicked continue to be praised even after their death. Whichever is chosen, the basic idea is clear.

THE PROBLEM OF DELAYED JUDGMENT

I hope the archaic and somewhat simple language of this passage does not make it difficult for new covenant believers to connect with it. Qohelet is reflecting on, affirming and helping us to be wise about a profound biblical truth which Old Testament wisdom literature in particular presents to us: we have everything to gain and everything to lose in the fear of the Lord. Neutrality is not possible; we will either treat God as God and trust and obey him as Lord, or treat him as an unreality and live according to our own best ideas – and die in our sins. Both Proverbs and Ecclesiastes promise the best of benefits to those who give themselves in reverent trust to the Lord, both in this life and in the next. But both books (and Ecclesiastes in particular) are quick to admit that these benefits do not always accrue quickly, easily or obviously. What God has twisted, none of us is able to straighten (1:15; 7:13). Qohelet is helping us towards the best kind of faith, which is as certain as Qohelet is about the final outcome (verse 13) while soberly realistic about how long it might take for that outcome to be realised. He is saving us from making a shipwreck of faith if our naïve expectations for this life are not realised in the ways we want. In this way, this passage comes close to the pastoral wisdom of 7:15–18.

Another way of saying this is to point to the tension in this passage, which is also present in 7:15–18: do wicked people enjoy long and full lives or not? Verse 12 seems to admit that this sometimes happens; verse 13 says it is an impossibility. Qohelet does not attempt to alleviate this problem, and neither should we. His wisdom can be utterly realistic about the world as it is without shaking his faith in God and the great worth of following him.

2. How to live well in light of delayed judgment • Ecclesiastes 8:14–15

So far, so good: we can be utterly realistic about the ways discipleship seems useless without giving up. But how do we make it through today, knowing that the fear of the Lord, although worth every sacrifice in the long run, will not necessarily guard us against the pain, distress, loss and darkness promised to those who give themselves to sin (verse 14)?[2]

Qohelet's answer is the same word of wisdom he has for us in every situation: there is nothing better for us (and, really, nothing else) than to receive everything God gives us under the sun (verse 15). Because we are unable to create the life we want for ourselves in the future, the only alternative is to enjoy life in the present as a gift: to eat, drink and enjoy our work. As in 2:10, the enjoyment we get from our work is our only takeaway, the only thing that will 'accompany' us from our work. Some great grief might meet us tomorrow, and all the piety in the world may not be able to stop it. But God has given us today. Wisdom receives, enjoys and leaves the future in God's hands (see 7:14).

It is worth pointing out that the word for 'enjoyment' here is the same as 'pleasure' in 2:1–3, where Qohelet wondered what use it was. Now he praises it, not because pleasure has changed, but because Qohelet has learned to receive it as a gift from God. Pleasure has no meaning aside from him.[3]

---

[2] In phrasing the issue this way, I have in mind the many verses in Proverbs that describe the dire fate of the wicked (e.g., 2:22; 3:25, 33; 4:19; 10:7, 28, 30; 11:5; 24:19–20).

[3] I am again grateful to my friend Joshua Knowles for pointing this out to me.

THE PROBLEM OF DELAYED JUDGMENT

3. *The mystery of providence* • *Ecclesiastes 8:16–17*

In verses 16–17, Qohelet draws a further separate conclusion about God's work from the problem of the delay of the benefits of fearing God (verses 10–14). As in 1:13, 16 and 7:25, Qohelet gave all of his considerable resources to understanding the nature of life under the sun ('on earth', verse 16), even depriving himself of sleep in his searching. He has already drawn a number of conclusions about what is good for human beings (2:3; 6:12). Now he turns away from what human beings should do in their lives under the sun to consider God's work in everything done in his world. As elsewhere, he draws a paradoxical conclusion, joining things he can see ('then I saw', verse 17) with many more things that escape him.

A quick observation about the NIV of verse 17 will help us appreciate the significance of what Qohelet is saying in this passage. The Hebrew literally reads, 'I saw all the work of God, that no man is able to find the work which is done under heaven.' The NIV takes the second phrase as referring to human work, which is entirely justifiable, given the use of 'the work done under heaven' with exactly this sense in 1:13 and 8:9. However, in this context, what is done under heaven seems to be God's work in the world, because the same word for 'work' or 'activity' refers to God's action in the first part of the verse. (Furthermore, Qohelet does know things about human work done under the sun, as he says in 1:14.)

In light of this, we should read the beginning of verse 17 as Qohelet's assurance that God is at work in everything, accomplishing his own will in and through everything that happens in the world. There is no time or place unimportant or distant to him. But exactly what God is doing is a complete mystery. Qohelet can see no larger order in the world's events which would reflect God's work in human history; he sees enough to know he cannot see the whole (compare 3:11). Neither can anyone else, no matter how hard they try – and anyone who claims to is either lying or deceived (verse 17). Anyone (Christian or not) who promises you *the* philosophy or life strategy to unlock life's mysteries and put you in a position to control your destiny does not know what they are talking about or is trying to trick you.

It is important we let the full force of this sink in. Ecclesiastes joins the rest of Scripture in unambiguously affirming God's limitless providential guiding of every inch of his creation ('all the work of God' in verse 17, my translation). All our days were written out in God's book ahead of time (Psalm 139:16); God fashions everything according to his proper purpose, even the wicked for the day of judgment (Proverbs 16:4). But the world does not give any evidence of such perfect guidance. To those of us living under the sun, Christians or not, the world mostly looks chaotic. In J. I. Packer's words, most of what happens under the sun bears 'no outward sign of a rational, moral God ordering them at all'.[4] Every once in a while, we get a hint of some larger beauty, some greater perfection which the divine author and symphony conductor summons together; most of the time we are completely in the dark. This is especially the case in relation to the urgent issue of the asymmetry between blessed wicked lives and painful righteous ones from verses 10–14. The same God who assures us that he is lovingly guiding every moment of our lives 'through thorny ways to a joyful end'[5] also assures us that we will never, in our earthly lives, see how (or we will only get rare glimpses). Real wisdom lies in acknowledging and accepting this – and turning to the enjoyment of the present task.

---

[4] Packer, *Knowing God*, 94.
[5] Kathrina von Schlegel (1697–1797), translated by Jane Borthwick (1813–97), 'Be Still, My Soul'. Public domain.

THE PROBLEM OF DELAYED JUDGMENT

REFLECTION

Instead of offering my own thoughts, I would like to quote from two Christians wiser than me who have helped me reflect on Ecclesiastes, especially with regard to passages like this.

First, pastor Zack Eswine, in a very astute guide to this book, relates a fascinating conversation he had with a fellow pastor friend.[6] They were admitting to each other how they constantly felt out of their depth in pastoral work, unsure what to say or how to proceed in the face of the deeply complex and painful problems that people would bring. They paused for a moment, and then asked each other why it would occur to them to feel bad about that. Why would they lament their limitations as a bad thing? Where does the desire to know everything come from, anyway (compare Genesis 3:5)? If we were to complain to God, 'Lord, I understand so little!' surely God would respond, 'Why is that a problem?'

Eswine relates how he and his friend laughed in relief as they realised how silly it was to be surprised or bothered that neither of them understood very much about what was happening around them. I think Qohelet would laugh in relief as well.

Second, Auca missionary and martyr Jim Elliot vividly expresses the kind of overwhelmedness which, although not a quotation from Ecclesiastes, is close to Qohelet's:

> My spirit is aruffle again at the vast, inexplicable complexities of humankind, and the careless, ineffective manner we fool 'fundamentalists' use in answering the cry of hearts which cannot understand themselves . . . The world, with its huge broil of minutiae, is within! Time with its tempest; space with its apparent infinitude, motion, change, that sense of 'something far more deeply interfused' . . . all these, and

---

[6] Zach Eswine, *Sensing Jesus: Life and Ministry as a Human Being* (Wheaton: Crossway, 2013), 36.

more. What can relate them and bring meaning to them all? Surely not our little church-goings and doctrine-learnings. It overwhelms me. I would despair indeed were it not for things like this: 'He is before all things, and in Him all things hold together' (Col 1:17).[7]

Note that Elliot is not saying that, because of the coherence of all things in Christ, the world snaps into an easily recognisable pattern. He allows both to stand: vast, inexplicable complexities together with gospel hope.

In Ecclesiastes, living wisely under the sun, before the eschaton, most importantly means receiving each day as a gift from God. Our present passage nuances and deepens our wisdom in receiving God's gift of earthly life. On the one hand, we know God is up to something profound and profoundly beautiful in our lives (1 Corinthians 2:9). On the other hand, wisdom accepts that we will never see what God is doing. There will never come a moment when your life will completely click into place and make perfect sense to you. In light of this limitation, there is nothing better than to enjoy today (verse 15).

---

[7] Elisabeth Elliot, *Shadow of the Almighty: The Life and Testament of Jim Elliot* (1958; reprint; Peabody, MA: Hendrickson, 2008), 102. The quotation is from Wordsworth's poem 'Tintern Abbey'.

12

Death as a Catalyst to Joy

ECCLESIASTES 9

Qohelet reflects simultaneously on the many things of which we cannot be certain, the one certainty we each have of death, and the simple joy of receiving our earthly lives as a gift.[1]

A common destiny for all

9 So I reflected on all this and concluded that the righteous and the wise and what they do are in God's hands, but no one knows whether love or hate awaits them. **2** All share a common destiny – the righteous and the wicked, the good and the bad,[a] the clean and the unclean, those who offer sacrifices and those who do not.

> As it is with the good,
>   so with the sinful;
> as it is with those who take oaths,
>   so with those who are afraid
>   to take them.

3 This is the evil in everything that happens under the sun: The same destiny overtakes all. The hearts of people, moreover, are full of evil and there is madness in their hearts while they live, and afterwards they join the dead. **4** Anyone who is among the living has hope[b] – even a live dog is better off than a dead lion!

> **5** For the living know that they will die,
>   but the dead know nothing;
> they have no further reward,
>   and even their name is
>   forgotten.
> **6** Their love, their hate
>   and their jealousy have long
>   since vanished;

---

[1] This summary is taken from Gibson, *Destiny*, 100–3.

never again will they have a part in anything that happens under the sun.

7 Go, eat your food with gladness, and drink your wine with a joyful heart, for God has already approved what you do. **8** Always be clothed in white, and always anoint your head with oil. **9** Enjoy life with your wife, whom you love, all the days of this meaningless life that God has given you under the sun – all your meaningless days. For this is your lot in life and in your toilsome labour under the sun. **10** Whatever your hand finds to do, do it with all your might, for in the realm of the dead, where you are going, there is neither working nor planning nor knowledge nor wisdom.

11 I have seen something else under the sun:

The race is not to the swift
> or the battle to the strong,
nor does food come to the wise
> or wealth to the brilliant
> or favour to the learned;
but time and chance happen to
> them all.

12 Moreover, no one knows when their hour will come:

As fish are caught in a cruel net,
> or birds are taken in a snare,
so people are trapped by evil
> times
> that fall unexpectedly upon
> them.

Wisdom better than folly

13 I also saw under the sun this example of wisdom that greatly impressed me: **14** there was once a small city with only a few people in it. And a powerful king came against it, surrounded it and built huge siege works against it. **15** Now there lived in that city a man poor but wise, and he saved the city by his wisdom. But nobody remembered that poor man. **16** So I said, 'Wisdom is better than strength.' But the poor man's wisdom is despised, and his words are no longer heeded.

17 The quiet words of the wise are
> more to be heeded
> than the shouts of a ruler of
> fools.
18 Wisdom is better than weapons
> of war,
> but one sinner destroys much
> good.

a 2 Septuagint (Aquila), Vulgate and Syriac; Hebrew does not have *and the bad*.

b 4 Or *What then is to be chosen? With all who live, there is hope*

1. Uncertainty in life and the certainty of death • Ecclesiastes 9:1–3

Verse 1 continues Qohelet's reflection from the previous chapter. Our lives and our achievements are entirely in God's hands; held in his loving care, but entirely at his disposal, not ours. Because of this, there simply is no telling what the future will bring.

In this verse, it is not immediately clear whether 'love' or 'hate' is divine or human. If we take the first option, some commentators wonder whether Qohelet is saying that it is impossible to know if we stand under God's favour or hatred. Qohelet repeats these two words in verse 6, however, where they clearly mean human love and hatred, and verse 7 shows that God's favour can be unambiguously enjoyed. So it is better to take 'love or hatred' as denoting our ignorance of whether our future will be lovely or hateful.

Qohelet turns from our uncertainty of the future (verse 1) to the one certainty we do have of our coming death (verses 2–3). He is not saying that righteousness and wickedness are meaningless and thus equally valid choices – he emphatically recommends righteousness, wisdom and the fear of the Lord as unqualifiedly better than their alternatives in light of God's judgment (2:13; 3:17; 5:6; 7:15–18; 8:12–13). But Qohelet will equally insist that even those who wisely give themselves to the fear of the Lord will end up in exactly the same place as those who ignore him (see 2:14–15; 3:19). Qohelet thinks it is absolutely better for us to fear God. He also looks us in the eye and bluntly tells us that nothing we do now will change that final end. The total effect of the different categories he invokes in verse 2 shows that every possible kind of person is included. This, too, the wise take to heart.

Compounding this gloomy reality is our despicable behaviour before we go to the dead (verse 3). If we would more closely attend to the meaning of a funeral (7:1–4), it might chasten and temper our pride and the brutality with which we treat others (3:18–19; 4:1). Instead, a self-aggrandising madness grips us – and we go to the grave regardless.

2. The preciousness of life • Ecclesiastes 9:4–6

Many would conclude from our lack of control in the present (verse 1) and our inescapable resting place in the grave (verses 2–3) that all the choices we make now are meaningless, even suicide. What difference can it make if I go to the grave now, by my own hand, as opposed to some years from now, unwillingly? We have already seen how Qohelet came to hate life because of death in 2:11, 17–23. But he has grown wiser by this point. Part of the great value of Ecclesiastes is that Qohelet says exactly the opposite of what we expect. This is because (as we will see) he has learned to factor God into the equation in a way most of us are not used to doing. Instead of concluding from the all-embracing reality of death that nothing matters, Qohelet engages in unrestrained rhetoric to convince us that the reality of death makes our lives right now incredibly precious. Even the most unimpressive, unattractive circumstances are still better than the grave: in the Old Testament, lions are the most impressive of animals, while dogs are unclean (verse 4).[2] Once you are in the grave, there is no more chance to participate

---

[2] Out of many possibilities, see the mention of dogs in Exodus 22:31; 1 Samuel 17:43; 24:14; 2 Samuel 9:8; 1 Kings 14:11; for lions, see Genesis 49:9; Numbers 23:24; Proverbs 28:1.

DEATH AS A CATALYST TO JOY

in anything life has to offer (verse 6), even if it is painful and unwelcome ('their hate'). Even knowing you are going to die is better than the opposite (verse 5). That is how much Qohelet values life.

It is only because Qohelet has taken the message of Death the Preacher so deeply to heart (7:1–4) that he gives this very unmodern statement of joy in life. The certainty of death, which drives many of us to gloom and even despair, pushes Qohelet in the opposite direction. He will reflect further on this in verses 7–9, a passage that forms the mirror image of verses 4–6, but before moving on, we should pause and consider the apparent contradiction between verses like Ecclesiastes 9:5 and the hope of the resurrection. 'The dead know nothing': it is easy to hear in statements like this a pagan pessimism, as if everyone is consigned to a vague and shadowy non-existence in the afterworld, far from God. In considering this, it is helpful to remember that Qohelet limits the whole of his investigation to life under the sun, before the eschaton, in the here and now. Ecclesiastes will end with the spirit returning to God (12:7) for judgment (verse 14); but he will not allow us any escape or distraction from how our earthly lives end, even theological ones. The resurrection happens only after the grave, and it is the grave that Qohelet wants us to think about.

This is confirmed by his use of the word *śākār* in verse 5, which means 'daily wage'. Qohelet is not denying any eschatological reward; he uses this word to speak only of what we get from our work in this life, and how we leave it behind in death. This passage should not be read as contradicting those parts of the Old Testament that speak unambiguously of fullness of life in God's presence after death (such as, Psalm 16:10; Job 19:25–7). Qohelet is speaking in verses 4–6 only of the pervasive reality of the grave and how to live wisely in light of it. It is as important to hear this as it is to hear the hope of the resurrection.

3. God already approves • Ecclesiastes 9:7–10

So far in this chapter, Qohelet has shown how the certainty of death (verses 2–3) makes the chance to participate in earthly life incredibly precious (verses 4–6). In verses 7–10, he returns to his favourite theme of enjoying daily life and work as a gift from God – but he overtops himself in his enthusiasm for the simple daily gifts of eating and working. The theme is familiar, but the passage oozes a zest and relish with which God's creatures should receive his gifts. The fact that he expresses himself in old covenant language and imagery (white clothes, oil on the head) should dull none of its excitement. It is meant to be almost overwhelming. If I can put it this way, this passage is Qohelet gripping our shoulders, shaking us, and saying, 'Today, today, God is giving to you to be alive! Woohoo!' Whatever we find to do today should be done with all our might, because there is soon coming a time when we will never again be able to go to work, see a sunset, play with our children or share a glass of wine with a friend (verse 10).

As throughout this book, this life is to be enjoyed not because it is meaningless, but because it is brief (verse 9). Unrestrained joy is the only wise response to life's brevity and our certain end in the grave. We have seen earlier how Qohelet will not let us take shelter in comforting lies about life under the sun. We see now how he also will not let us sink into self-pity. Will we treat God's gifts as if they were nothing, just because they do not last forever?

One more thing to note: verse 7 is probably the clearest statement of the gospel in Ecclesiastes. 'God has already approved what you do.' God is *already* happy with our work and limited accomplishments, already approving and delighting in them, irrespective of what we do or do not accomplish in this life, and irrespective of the fact that (from an 'under-the-sun' perspective) we accomplish nothing permanent. Of course, 'work' here means the daily grind of your job, not religious 'good works' which are excluded from justification by faith (Galatians 2:16). But there is a consonance in the ideas. God accepts and approves of people irrespective of (religious) good works or accomplishment in earthly endeavours; he smiles on us, irrespective of human achievement (religious or occupational).

For those unused to the thought, God's disregard of our achievements can be insulting. But for those who accept their total need before the righteous Judge, as well as their total inability to create anything of permanence in their working life, the thought is deeply liberating.[3] The next time you go to your place of work, picture your heavenly Father smiling at you before you get anything done, and see for yourself the difference it makes.[4]

4. Uncertainty, death and the limitations of wisdom • Ecclesiastes 9:11–18

We have seen above how Qohelet presents the enjoyment of life as a strategy that allows us to negotiate the realities of life under the sun without delivering us from brevity and vanity. Qohelet repeats this here, twice referring to (literally) 'your *hebel*-life' in verse 9, and following up a passage of unrestrained eagerness for daily life (verses 7–10) with the uncertainty of our lives now (verse 11) and our lack of control (verse 12). Verse 11 is a near-perfect definition of *hebel*/'vanity': effect and cause do not line up; try as we might, we cannot predict or control outcomes. Furthermore, we cannot resist or even predict misfortune and loss (verse 12; compare 7:14). 'Evil times' in verse 12 is actually

---

[3] I have tried to spell this out in more depth in 'The Gospel in the Book of Ecclesiastes', *Journal of the Evangelical Theological Society* 56 (2013): 697–706.

[4] Qohelet is describing all different kinds of work here. The verse does not apply to people who (for instance) make money as criminals.

singular, and probably includes death without being limited to it ('when their hour will come'). This is part of biblical wisdom. 'We tend to live as if the one thing which is certain will never come, while the many things which are uncertain are certain,' as Gibson puts it.[5]

An example that demonstrates verses 11–12 follows in verses 13–18. Qohelet has already said that one wise man is stronger than ten generals (7:19); now he narrates how a single wise man saved a city from certain defeat (verses 13–15), but was ignored in the end (verse 15). That wise man could not win for himself the glorious future among his fellows that he deserved. The race truly does not belong to the swift (verse 11).

Qohelet then reflects in verses 16–18 on the great value of wisdom, together with the grievous way in which it is ignored. It accomplishes so much, but is destroyed so easily (verse 18).

REFLECTION

There is coming a time when you will see the sun for the last time. You will taste food for the last time. You will feel the touch of your spouse or your family for the last time. You will take your last breath.

It may be as you lie in a hospital bed, waiting for the end. It may take you entirely by surprise: an accident, a stroke. You may go to sleep and simply never wake up.

You do not know when or how, but we both know this is coming. It could be decades from now; it might happen before you put this book down.

Paul beautifully writes of how 'our light and momentary troubles' are working for us 'an eternal glory that far outweighs them all' (2 Corinthians 4:17). Not just 'compensates', but 'outweighs', 'far outweighs'. One sip from the water of life, one taste from the tree of life (Revelation 22:1–2), and every meal you ever ate,

---

[5] Gibson, *Destiny*, 103.

no matter how succulent, will be utterly forgotten. One look at the face of Christ (Revelation 22:4), and any memory of the warmth of the sun will fade to nothing. One embrace of your divine Husband will cure whatever heartbreak and heartache you suffered, whatever years of loneliness you endured.

I wait for all these things with 'eager expectation' (Romans 8:19). We will not be hankering for our old lives when we awake in Christ's likeness (Psalm 17:15). But that does not mean we should despise the sun now, letting our food be tasteless or friendships grow cold. The time quickly comes when we will lose them all. This is not ultimate loss. But God expects us to treat this world as 'good', even 'very good' (Genesis 1:31). I will not be crushed with grief when I take my last walk in a forest or read *The Lord of the Rings* for the last time. But it will be a poignant goodbye for me.

13

Various Proverbs

ECCLESIASTES 10

This chapter is the one place in the book where Qohelet sounds most like the book of Proverbs. Each individual statement is relevant to the book's main theme: even though we are ignorant of the future and not in control of it (verse 14), wisdom is still possible for those living under the sun. The varied situations Qohelet addresses make any outline of this chapter difficult.

10 As dead flies give perfume a bad smell,
 so a little folly outweighs wisdom and honour.
2 The heart of the wise inclines to the right,
 but the heart of the fool to the left.
3 Even as fools walk along the road,
 they lack sense
 and show everyone how stupid they are.
4 If a ruler's anger rises against you,
 do not leave your post;
 calmness can lay great offences to rest.

5 There is an evil I have seen under the sun,
 the sort of error that arises from a ruler:
6 fools are put in many high positions,
 while the rich occupy the low ones.
7 I have seen slaves on horseback,
 while princes go on foot like slaves.

8 Whoever digs a pit may fall into it;
 whoever breaks through a wall may be bitten by a snake.
9 Whoever quarries stones may be

injured by them;
>   whoever splits logs may be endangered by them.

10 If the axe is dull
>   and its edge unsharpened,
> more strength is needed,
>   but skill will bring success.

11 If a snake bites before it is charmed,
>   the charmer receives no fee.

12 Words from the mouth of the wise are gracious,
>   but fools are consumed by their own lips.

13 At the beginning their words are folly;
>   at the end they are wicked madness —

14   and fools multiply words.

No one knows what is coming —
>   who can tell someone else what will happen after them?

15 The toil of fools wearies them;
>   they do not know the way to town.

16 Woe to the land whose king was a servant[a]
>   and whose princes feast in the morning.

17 Blessed is the land whose king is of noble birth
>   and whose princes eat at a proper time —
> for strength and not for drunkenness.

18 Through laziness, the rafters sag;
>   because of idle hands, the house leaks.

19 A feast is made for laughter,
>   wine makes life merry,
> and money is the answer for everything.

20 Do not revile the king even in your thoughts,
>   or curse the rich in your bedroom,
> because a bird in the sky may carry your words,
>   and a bird on the wing may report what you say.

---

a 16 Or *king is a child*

VARIOUS PROVERBS

1. Wisdom precious and vulnerable • Ecclesiastes 10:1

The first verse of this chapter complements the last verse of chapter 9: precious as wisdom is, it is easily spoiled. Remembering the realities of daily hygiene in ancient Israel (no showers, no deodorant) will suggest the pungency this metaphor would have had for the book's first audience.

2. The wise and fools distinguish themselves • Ecclesiastes 10:2–3

Qohelet has already written at length about how everyone eventually winds up in the same place, irrespective of the quality of the life they lived (2:14–15; 9:2–3). In spite of this, the wise and the foolish obviously distinguish themselves during their lives. Fools cannot hide who they really are. It is worth reading this in connection with warnings in Proverbs that sometimes malicious people can pass themselves off as friends to those walking the way of wisdom (for example, 26:24–5), but eventually the truth comes out (for example, Proverbs 10:9).

3. Faithfulness in service • Ecclesiastes 10:4

Qohelet then returns to the subject of wise service to the throne (verse 4). As in 8:2–6, submissive faithfulness is key, even when someone with the authority to destroy you is angry. This verse applies whether the anger is justified or not. 'Calmness' especially means soothing speech. In Proverbs 15:4, the same word is used to speak of how a soothing tongue is a tree of life; in Proverbs 16:14, the wise know how to appease the deadly anger of the king. The wise know how to defuse and calm the anger of their superiors, whether justly provoked or not.

4. Unworthy leaders • Ecclesiastes 10:5–7

Qohelet then turns to a painful situation he witnessed: rulers who elevate the unworthy to positions of promise and demote those most deserving (verses 5–7; compare Proverbs 19:10). 'Rich' here means not the rapacious and dishonest gaining of wealth, but wise stewards of money who know how to use a position of authority to benefit others; similarly, 'slaves' is best taken not as victims of trafficking but debtors or those with a criminal record. In Zach Eswine's words, 'An erring leader overlooks . . . faithful character [revealed in good stewardship of money] and places impatient, wandering, slothful, get-rich-quick schemers tragically in charge.'[1] But this is evil (verse 5) and benefits no one.

5. Unpredictability and industry • Ecclesiastes 10:8–11

Verses 8–9 give a series of examples of what Qohelet has already described in 9:11: cause and effect do not always line up. In normal conditions, of course, digging a pit or splitting a log is not dangerous. One has to earn a living somehow, and Old Testament wisdom continually commends hard work (see verse 18 below, as well as, for example, Proverbs 10:4; 14:23). But we are not sovereign over our lives. We cannot automatically secure beneficial outcomes even in normal circumstances and should not be vexed when unfortunate surprises meet us (see 7:9, 13).

But the screwy unpredictability of life under the sun is no excuse for sloppy work (verse 10). Skill sharpens the axe, even when bludgeoning your way through might eventually reach the same outcome. Caution and skill can help you avoid potential harm (verse 11).

Qohelet's examples of swinging axes and charming snakes

---

[1] Eswine, *Recovering Eden*, 198. Eswine's discussion of this chapter is very helpful.

might not have the purchase in our imaginations that they would have had for ancient Israelites, but there is nothing really new under the sun. It is possible for those living 'under the sun' to expect their work always to succeed quickly and easily, and then be shocked and impatient when *hebel* gets in the way.[2] This impatience can be intolerant of fatigue in others (including the staff of one's church), always pushing people and never giving them time to rest, recover and regain their sharpness. This kind of leader has 'no category for taking a long view by going slow, taking strategic rest, and spending a day doing nothing but attending to the boring and humdrum necessity of sharpening tools. They are entertained and dazzled by fly-by-night flashes.'[3] This kind of leader can be superficially impressive, but cannot get long-term results. If you never pull back and restrategise (i.e., ask what needs to be sharpened), you will (at best) wear yourself and others out. At worst, you will bring injury on yourself and others, like someone drawing the attention of a dangerous animal without having the skill to handle it (verse 11).[4]

6. *Wise and foolish speech* • *Ecclesiastes 10:12–15*

Qohelet then turns to the very common wisdom theme of wise and foolish speech (verses 12–15), joining it to his repeated reflections on our ignorance of the future and inability to control it (verse 14). It is this the fool ignores – he talks and talks, but never submits to the limitations God has placed on life under the sun. This leads him into all kinds of craziness (13b) which eventually destroys him (12b). Wise people might be tired at the end of a day's work, but since they accept brevity and vanity,

---

[2] Eswine, *Recovering Eden*, 201.
[3] Eswine, *Recovering Eden*, 202.
[4] See further Eswine, *Recovering Eden*, 203.

they can enjoy work as a divine gift and rest in the evening; the fool's presumption means all his work is a weariness (14a), and he cannot even find his way home when the day is done (14b). This is what comes of speaking and planning as if God has not subjected creation to frustration.

The kind of speech which Qohelet diagnoses as foolish in this passage can appear in church. Sometimes church members want everything to work all the time – they never acknowledge any limits.[5] Sometimes church leaders foolishly overestimate their ability to plan and control the future, ignoring how Ecclesiastes teaches that we simply cannot anticipate what tomorrow will bring.[6] No matter how superficially impressive, leaders of this sort run the risk of ruining themselves and their churches.

By way of contrast, wise speech is gracious (12a); the same root is used in Proverbs for mercy (21:10) and kindness to the needy (14:21, 31). It is easy to think of a number of ways in which wise speech might be gracious, of course, but since the context shows a contrast with foolish presumption about life under the sun, this wise speech is probably gracious in that it accepts the limitations God has placed on his earthly gifts. This speech does not break people with impossible expectations. It is life-giving in its realistic acceptance of vanity and brevity, and calls others to enjoy life within (and because of) these boundaries.

7. Unwise leadership • Ecclesiastes 10:16–17

Qohelet returns to royal rule in verses 16–17. The 'woe' beginning verse 16 is meant to sting: this is a miniature lament over the suffering caused by unwise leadership which abuses its privileges in constant self-indulgence. The Ugandan proverb, 'Without a

---

[5] Eswine, *Recovering Eden*, 203.
[6] Eswine, *Recovering Eden*, 205.

leader, the ants are confused,' exposes the same problem.[7] How much better those noble-minded rulers who plan even their meals so they can rule well.[8]

8. Laziness and laughter • Ecclesiastes 10:18–19

Qohelet sounds the common wisdom theme of the dangers of laziness next (verse 18). He has laboured hard in this book to impress upon us the need for realistic expectations about work (something he learned to his own grief, as he narrates in 2:1–11). But the realities of life under the sun are no excuse for loafing, which only hurts you.

At the same time, the danger of laziness should not push us to thoughtless, stressful overwork, because life is meant to be enjoyed (verse 19). We should remember here the 'high achievers' we met in chapters 5–6 who wear themselves out without ever asking why they do it (see 5:10–17; 6:3). This is true even for money. The NIV's 'money is the answer for everything' is a valid translation and can be taken as a sad admission of how money makes life better even for unscrupulous people (compare Proverbs 17:8). However, I think a better translation is 'money occupies everyone' or 'keeps everyone busy', and not in a bad sense.[9] We enjoy our food and the friends we eat with, as well as pleasant occupations which allow us to make some kind of living for ourselves (compare 5:19–20).

---

[7] Habtu, 'Ecclesiastes', in *Africa Bible Commentary*, 794.
[8] Eswine, *Recovering Eden*, 207.
[9] Three homonyms coming in the verbal root *'nh*: 'to answer', 'to be humble' or 'to be troubled about or busy with'. Qohelet uses the root in the last sense three times earlier (1:13; 3:10; 5:19), making it more likely (to my mind) that that is the sense here.

9. Do not criticise • Ecclesiastes 10:20

Restraint in speech closes the chapter in verse 20. Harbouring criticism of a leader, chewing on your frustrations and giving a lot of mental space to them, is dangerous because it is so difficult to keep them hidden — even if they are justified. Your frustrations will all too easily colour your speech and become known, to your own hurt. Qohelet is consistent in his advocation of restraint, submission and faithful work, irrespective of the moral qualities of the authority you serve. Two helpful biblical examples of this are Daniel serving under Nebuchadnezzar and Mordecai serving King Ahasuerus. Neither king is a moral exemplar, but both Daniel and Mordecai show exemplary work regardless.

REFLECTION

I remarked above how humble Qohelet's wisdom is in chapter 4. The same word seems appropriate for this chapter. Although he makes wide-ranging investigations into the nature of life under the sun (1:13, 17; 7:25), Qohelet also helps us think through the best ways to negotiate the most ordinary of situations. The wisdom that accepts all of life from God's hand will also accept and apply these wise words with equal joy.

14

Generous Work Before a Cosmic Funeral

ECCLESIASTES 11:1–12:8

Qohelet's wisdom about enjoying life and facing the realities of brevity and vanity reaches a dual climax. He first gives his most enthusiastic statement of his main theme: unrestrained engagement with life through hard work, despite our ignorance of what will succeed and what will not (11:1–6). He then makes a call to remember (11:7–12:8) both the coming days of darkness (11:8) and our Creator when we are young (12:1). These two passages belong together, for it is only an unflinching view of one's end (11:7–12:8) that can create the capacity to fully and deeply enjoy God's gift of life (11:1–6).

1. Work! Risk! Be generous! • Ecclesiastes 11:1–6

Invest in many ventures

11 Ship your grain across the sea;
   after many days you may
      receive a return.
2 Invest in seven ventures, yes, in
      eight;
   you do not know what
      disaster may come upon
      the land.

3 If clouds are full of water,
   they pour rain on the earth.
Whether a tree falls to the south
      or to the north,
   in the place where it falls,
      there it will lie.
4 Whoever watches the wind will
      not plant;
   whoever looks at the clouds
      will not reap.

> ⁵ As you do not know the path of the wind,
>   or how the body is formedᵃ in a mother's womb,
> so you cannot understand the work of God,
>   the Maker of all things.
>
> ⁶ Sow your seed in the morning, and at evening let your hands not be idle,
>   for you do not know which will succeed,
>   whether this or that, or whether both will do equally well.

ᵃ 5 Or *know how life* (or *the spirit*) / *enters the body being formed*

The NIV's rendering of verses 1–2 reflects a possible interpretation of these verses, but masks the actual wording of the text. A more literal translation would read:

> Send your bread upon the face of the waters,
>   for after many days you may find it;
> give a portion to seven, also to eight,
>   for you do not know what disaster will come
>   upon the earth.

Some commentators have seen a recommendation of maritime investment here, as reflected in the NIV.[1] But it is strange to have so specific a venture recommended at such a climactic place in the book, especially when only a few would be rich enough to do this, and Qohelet normally recommends enjoying life in a way which everyone can do, rich or poor. This also strains the Hebrew: Qohelet says you may find only what you sent, not make a return (verse 1); and never elsewhere in the Old Testament does 'to give a portion' mean 'make an investment'.[2]

It is better to take verses 1–2 as a summons to generosity, even

---

[1] See Seow, *Ecclesiastes*, 341, along with criticisms of this reading on 341–4, as well as Fox, *A Time to Tear Down*, 311–14.
[2] See *nātan* with *ḥēleq* in Joshua 14:4; 15:13; Ecclesiastes 2:21.

when there seems to be no benefit. Since seven is the number of perfection and completion in the Old Testament, this is a call for unrestrained generosity. The imagery of 'sending bread' confirms the sense of giving money away in situations where you do not immediately stand to benefit: the bread here is thin, round pittas that might float for a while. The verb used can also mean to release or let something go.[3]

Two reasons are given to do this: it may unexpectedly benefit the giver (verse 1), and hardship may make charity impossible in the future (verse 2). This potential future disaster might be one that falls on the one receiving charity (making our present generosity even more urgent), but it may equally fall on the giver. Since we might be in our grave by this time tomorrow, we may not have the chance to be generous later and so should do as much as possible for the needy now.[4]

It is important not to miss that risk and the unpredictability of life are not reasons to hold on to our money, but are themselves reasons to give it away. Qohelet's wisdom is continually and helpfully counter-intuitive.

As he usually does, Qohelet proceeds to nuance his previous statement without withdrawing it. The possible future benefit of charity should give no hope of escaping unpredictability and manipulating life to our advantage. Some of the patterns God has set up in creation benefit humanity, such as rain; but some are indifferent – falling trees that just lie there (verse 3). The world is not random chaos, but not everything happens because of us or for us. Wisdom accepts these limitations.

A further nuance is given in verse 4: the fact that we cannot control very much and that some patterns in creation do not benefit us is not meant to paralyse. If we stare like a deer into headlights at the things we cannot control, we will accomplish nothing.

---

[3] See the Piel of *šālah* in Deuteronomy 24:4; Judges 12:9; 15:5; 1 Samuel 24:20.
[4] Gibson, *Destiny*, 120–21.

Qohelet then gives a final statement of his repeated admonition to work with all our might while we live (9:10) and to enjoy our work to the fullest (5:18) in verses 5–6. There is still no escape from *hebel* here; effect and cause still do not always line up (9:11), such that we do not know what will flourish and what will wither, regardless of how hard we work. But the enthusiasm of these two verses is palpable. Qohelet even spins *hebel* in our favour at the end of verse 6: just because we cannot predict the future, everything we put our hand to might work out unexpectedly well.

Deepening the hopefulness of this passage is the way Qohelet connects our work with God's. (The NIV's rendering of the ending of verse 5 obscures this; instead of 'Maker of all things', Qohelet says God 'does all things' – that is, he is at work in everything.[5]) Qohelet has already made the connection between our work and God's in 8:16–17, but he leveraged it to emphasise our epistemological limits. The same connection is made in 11:5–6, but now it becomes a motivation to hard work. Just because God is at work in everything (verse 5), both evening and morning should find us diligently plugging away (verse 6). Whether we succeed or fail, God is at work in everything. The fact that we have no idea what God is accomplishing in our work does not mean he is absent.

The metaphor of new life in the womb is also a remarkably happy one for the manner of God's work in the world in and through our work. Infant mortality rates in the ancient world were tragically high (at least at 50 per cent). Furthermore, ancient Israelites would have known less about conception and pregnancy than we do: sometimes a couple could get pregnant and sometimes not; no one would have understood why, and childless couples had no other medical recourse. As a result, the conception and birth of a

---

[5] 'Maker' would be the participle of the verb instead of the imperfect, as in Isaiah 51:13.

new baby would have been the most happy and most mysterious of gifts – and that is the way God is at work in all things, quickening new life where we cannot control outcomes. It is just for this reason that we should work hard at everything. Who knows what new life God is bringing about through our daily tasks?

I hope it is obvious how far away Qohelet is from the despair and hatred of life in chapter 2. He has learned how to be utterly realistic about life under the sun and utterly joyful in it, and invites us into the same. This is wisdom which is as rare as it is precious.

2. A cosmic funeral • Ecclesiastes 11:7–12:8

Ecclesiastes is centrally concerned with both the grim realities of life under the sun and the possibility of joyful engagement with this life. Far from excluding each other, Qohelet thinks that we can only truly enjoy life once we face its brevity and vanity, and, indeed, it is just exactly brevity and vanity that put us in a position to receive life as a gift. Having spoken to joyful engagement with life in 11:1–6, he turns to his other major theme and brings our quickly approaching death to our attention. As above, this common theme receives a heightened and climactic expression. This passage is structured according to two calls to remember (in verse 8, governing 11:7–10, and in 12:1, governing 12:1–8).

Remembering the days of darkness as an incentive to joy (11:7–10)

Remember your Creator while young
⁷ Light is sweet,
    and it pleases the eyes to see the sun.

⁸ However many years anyone may live,
    let them enjoy them all.
But let them remember the days of darkness,

for there will be many.
Everything to come is
   meaningless.

9 You who are young, be happy
   while you are young,
   and let your heart give you
   joy in the days of your
   youth.
Follow the ways of your heart
and whatever your eyes see,
but know that for all these things
   God will bring you into
   judgment.

10 So then, banish anxiety from
   your heart
and cast off the troubles of
   your body,
for youth and vigour are
   meaningless.

Taken out of context, verse 7 is jejune; but when we remember that the person saying this is the same one who hated and despaired over life in chapter 2, it takes on poignant depth. Sometimes the most profound insights are the simplest. Being happy just to see the sun is no small thing.

Verse 8 gives the reason: every single day is to be enjoyed, because the days of darkness are soon coming. Even if our days are many, no boredom should dampen our joy, no weary fatigue at having seen it all. The 'but' beginning the command to remember in verse 8 is a valid translation, but I think Qohelet's thought is better represented by the translation, '*And* remember,' for our knowledge of our death is not held in spite of our joy in life, but is a catalyst for it.[6] This enjoyment is not the mindless distraction against which Qohelet warned us in 7:1–6, but solid joy in God's earthly gifts before they are gone. The 'vanity' to come at the end of verse 8 is described further in 12:1–8.

It is important to remember that, in the Old Testament, 'remembering' does not mean recalling something that slipped your mind, but dwelling in the reality of something. For example, 'remembering' the Sabbath (Exodus 20:8) does not imply that ancient Israelites had to be reminded not to work on Saturday.

---

[6] The connective *vav* in Hebrew can mean either 'and' or 'but'.

The fourth commandment calls for deeply embracing and celebrating the reality of God's liberation of them by resting. In light of this, 'remembering' the days of darkness calls for an unblinking, sober recognition of death, your death, as the most solid reason to enjoy life now. Qohelet guides us away from both a despair that withdraws and a despair that distracts by gorging itself (1 Corinthians 15:32, quoting Isaiah 22:13). God does not give the gifts of life and work to everyone, and he will not give them to us forever.

The call to enjoy intensifies in verses 9–10 but is specifically applied to the young (verse 9), because youth is so brief (verse 10; as argued above, 'meaningless' will not work as a translation because something being meaningless cannot stand as a reason to enjoy it).[7] Qohelet piles term upon term for expansive enjoyment in everything life has to offer. Engage in whatever kind of activity appeals to you (see 1:13; 5:19); follow wherever your heart leads! The 'anxiety' that should be avoided (verse 10) recalls the use of the same word in 2:23 (there translated as 'grief'), where Qohelet narrated how his enjoyment of life collapsed. It is a way of hinting to the young man not to repeat Qohelet's mistake, but rather to receive this fleeting life as a gift.[8]

In fact, it is a gift that God insists on. As in verse 8, it is valid to translate the end of verse 9 as a restrictive caution: enjoy everything, except for sin which will invite God's judgment. Certainly, Qohelet would agree with this (7:17; 8:13). But it is equally valid to translate: 'Rejoice, enjoy, follow, and know that for all these things God will bring you into judgment' – in the sense that failure to enjoy earthly life is a culpable mistake that

---

[7] NIV's 'vigour' in verse 10 is an interpretative take on a difficult word; *šahărût* might be derived from the root 'to be black' or related to the word 'dawn'. Either or both is possible: youth as the dawn of life, before your hair goes white (in Proverbs 20:29, grey hair stands for old age).

[8] Gibson wisely points out that, if you labour under the illusion that you can control life, anxiety will consume you; *Destiny*, 137.

can incur God's anger. If taken this way, the final line is not a restriction but another reason to enjoy life. However counter-intuitive this might seem, I think it fits best with the expansive joy of the passage.[9] Biblically speaking, part of fearing God involves relishing even his earthly gifts and having a fantastic time when we are young.[10] Anything less is disobedience. Self-pity, grouchiness and vexation over how we cannot control our lives or accomplish anything permanent are as much a denial of our Creator's purposes for us as transgressing his other commands.[11] As Gibson says:

> There are better things to do than succeed, more important things to do than to make it in the world, and there are worse things to do than fail . . . A life fully lived is a life receiving the reward of today as a gift that you don't deserve and one that God has given you to enjoy.[12]

---

[9] It seems to have been counter-intuitive to ancient readers of Ecclesiastes as well; one of the Greek translations of the book adds to the middle line of the verse, 'Walk in the ways of your heart blameless, and not in the sight of your eyes.' It has the effect of weakening the command to enjoy to a grudging allowance: 'Enjoy yourself, but you had better not sin!' Such narrowness can feel spiritual, but it wanders from the very commands it presumes to guard.

[10] Will Kynes gives a very appropriate quote from the Talmud in relation to this verse: 'Everyone must give an account before God of all things one saw in life and did not enjoy'; *Qiddushin* 4:12, quoted in Will Kynes, 'Follow Your Heart and Do Not Say It Was a Mistake: Qoheleth's Allusions to Numbers 15 and the Story of the Spies', in *Reading Ecclesiastes Intertextually*, ed. Katharine Dell and Will Kynes (London: Bloomsbury, 2016), 19. His discussion is fascinating, especially with regard to the relationship between this verse and the similar phrasing for the spies roving through the Promised Land in Numbers 15:39; he argues that this connection was articulated by the rabbis in a way that does not quite account for the unrestricted joy in which it is expressed.

[11] Gibson, *Destiny*, 136.

[12] Gibson, *Destiny*, 121, 124.

GENEROUS WORK BEFORE A COSMIC FUNERAL

Remember your Creator before the days of darkness (12:1–8)

12 Remember your Creator
   in the days of your youth,
before the days of trouble come
   and the years approach when
      you will say,
   'I find no pleasure in them' –
2 before the sun and the light
   and the moon and the stars
      grow dark,
   and the clouds return after
      the rain;
3 when the keepers of the house
      tremble,
   and the strong men stoop,
   when the grinders cease because
      they are few,
   and those looking through
      the windows grow dim;
4 when the doors to the street are
      closed
   and the sound of grinding
      fades;
   when people rise up at the
      sound of birds,
   but all their songs grow faint;
5 when people are afraid of heights
      and of dangers in the streets;
   when the almond tree blossoms
   and the grasshopper drags
      itself along
   and desire no longer is
      stirred.
Then people go to their eternal
      home
   and mourners go about the
      streets.

6 Remember him – before the
      silver cord is severed,
   and the golden bowl is
      broken;
before the pitcher is shattered at
      the spring,
   and the wheel broken at the
      well,
7 and the dust returns to the
      ground it came from,
   and the spirit returns to God
      who gave it.

8 'Meaningless! Meaningless!' says
      the Teacher.[a]
   'Everything is meaningless!'

---

a 8 Or *the leader of the assembly*; also in verses 9 and 10

Qohelet turns to describe those many days of deep darkness from 11:8. The key command in this passage is given only once:

to remember the God who made us (verse 1), before the days of darkness come ('before' repeats three times in verses 1, 2, 6). The full nuance of 'remembering' is at play here. Qohelet calls us to fear, reverence, obey and remain loyal to our Creator while we are still young, before our potential and ability to enjoy life dry up (verse 1b).

Have you noticed how young people are delighted with everyday occurrences which adults hardly notice? Children splash in the bath, throw snowballs, jump in puddles; teenagers listen to the latest bands, make their own music, play sports . . . and adults trudge to the office. Young people have a capacity to engage with life in its newness which fades with time. Soon enough the younger generation will replace their parents at work, however, and life will not taste quite the same – but all the while, young people will have been creating the kinds of lives they either enjoy or endure until the grave. The very quality of youth is to feel it will last forever because you have nothing with which to contrast it. A young person may not realise they can sin in such a way that leaves a permanently sour taste as they enter adulthood. Remembering God as God in your youth sets up a much happier trajectory and creates a much happier mental and spiritual environment for one to live in as the years pass.[13] As elsewhere in Ecclesiastes, pleasure and enjoyment turn bitter without God (compare 2:1–3). This means that there is a warning against sin in this passage, but it comes in 12:1, not 11:7–10.

Qohelet then expands in verses 2–5 on the 'days of darkness' which will meet each of us when youth and life leave us. These verses form the background of our need to remember God early in life (verse 1). It is one of the most mysterious and (to me) alluring passages in all of Scripture. The images are arresting, but what do they mean? Why is it important to remember God before the clouds return after rain (verse 2),

---

[13] Gibson is very good on this; see *Destiny*, 143–5.

or the doors in the street are shut (verse 4), with dangers in the street (verse 5)?

One interpretation, which has a very long pedigree, takes the images allegorically to represent the body breaking down in old age and death.[14] According to this interpretation, the grinders are teeth, those looking through windows are eyes that grow dim (verse 3), songs growing faint refers to a quaking, weak voice (verse 4), and so on. This interpretation is entirely possible, but it is not without problems. For example, allegorists cannot agree on what each image represents: are 'the keepers of the house' in verse 3 ribs? Or hands? Or something else?[15] Does the darkening sun represent eyes growing dim, or fading enjoyment of life? Michael Fox lists multiple possible allegorical readings of each image, none more convincing than the others.[16] It is difficult to avoid a sense of arbitrariness in this kind of approach. Furthermore, some images do not obviously connect with an aging and dying body. It is hard to make sense of the clouds returning after rain from this perspective; and the fear beginning verse 5 presumably refers literally to a feeling of vulnerability and feebleness in old age, not allegorically to a part of the body. If this passage were intended to be an allegory, surely it would have been clearer?

These problems suggest that an allegorical way of reading Ecclesiastes 12 is on the wrong track. An allegory intends the reader to move past the visible surface of the text to the abstract meanings that stand behind the narrative. In John Bunyan's *Pilgrim's Progress*, for example, it is not swamps in themselves that matter when Christian falls into the Slough of Despond, but the

---

[14] The normally literal Syriac translation switches to full-blown allegory here. Rashi, Rashbam and Joseph Qara' follow the same line; Cohen (ed.), *Miqra'ot Gedolot HaKeter*, 204–8. Gibson is a modern representative; *Destiny*, 138–40.

[15] Michael Fox lists multiple possibilities (ribs, hands, knees, arms, legs) in the history of interpretation of this passage; *A Time to Tear Down*, 344–5.

[16] Fox, *A Time to Tear Down*, 344–5.

way a swamp evokes some part of the Christian journey. But perhaps we are not meant to look through the images of 12:2–5 to some other meaning standing behind them. Perhaps we are meant to dwell within the images and let them go to work on our imaginations. Perhaps they are not meant to communicate information but evoke a certain atmosphere.[17] Let us try the passage from this perspective.[18] For the moment, do not worry if the images do not entirely make sense or cohere very well. Let's listen and follow the words.[19]

Imagine yourself standing just outside the town where you have always lived, standing on solid earth, under the sun – the same earth which has stood for generations (1:4). Eclipse-like, the sun darkens. The luminous moon shades to black; you cannot even see its outline. One by one the stars wink out. The massive dome of the sky above you is dark, utterly dark.

---

[17] As mentioned, Michael Fox has a superb discussion of this passage and different ways to make sense of it; *A Time to Tear Down*, 344–5, 333–49.

[18] Sometimes music helps. If you want, find the choral piece 'For Whom the Bell Tolls', by Steve Baker and Carmen Daye, and listen as you read; or the last movement of Gustav Mahler's Ninth Symphony. Both are superb evocations of the atmosphere of this passage.

[19] You will notice that my comments below sometimes differ from the NIV. Since I want you to read the next paragraph uninterruptedly, let me give some guidance about how I read these verses before we enter them. First, I connect the clouds in verse 2 with the rainclouds of 11:3 because Qohelet says the clouds 'return' (apparently they were here before). But it seems that these returning clouds are now ominous storm clouds (as in Judges 5:4; Psalm 18:11–12; 77:17). Second, the NIV renders the last line in verse 3 as 'those looking through the windows grow dim', but the verb is actually 'grow dark' (the same verb for the sun growing dark in verse 2). Third, the NIV mistranslates 'caperberry' as 'desire' (verse 5); the word *'ăbîyônāh* refers to a caper plant. 'Desire' is normally expressed by *těšûqāh* (such as in Song of Songs 7:10) or *ta'ăbāh* (as in Psalm 119:20). The NIV translators were probably influenced by the allegorical interpretation of this passage, which often takes this as an image of failing sexual potency (among other options; see further Fox, *A Time to Tear Down*, 345).

Storm clouds gather above you. It rained earlier (see 11:3), and you were glad; the farmers needed it. Now they rumble darkly, deep with thunder. You look towards your town and see the men who guarded the city gates trembling; strong men, normally unafraid of whoever they meet, now twist themselves, stoop and seem unable to walk upright. The normal sound of daily work has stopped: no more grinding of wheat, with women singing as they work; and it is not until you hear the unearthly silence that you realise what a comfort the background hum of daily activity was.[20] Door after door shuts; shadows are cast on those looking through windows. You notice ravens settling on every roof, jet-black, cawing. People look around furtively and give nervous glances at the sky. Strangely, in all the atmosphere of gloom, the almond tree in the town square is blossoming in brilliant white; but you can see an insect dragging itself along its bark, and next to it, a caperberry tree lies broken.

You see all the town assembled, dressed in black; not a few faces show tears, and a mournful song sounds. They walk through the town following a coffin. You realise everything has shut down for a funeral. You look in the coffin. The dead face, eyes closed . . . is your own. You are witnessing your own funeral. 'People go to their eternal home, and mourners go about the streets' (verse 5).[21]

It is not until the end of verse 5 that the confusing, surreal

---

[20] Fox, *A Time to Tear Down*, 333.

[21] It is just as well that the reader knows that a number of other translations of verse 5 are possible. Qohelet literally says that the almond tree causes disgust (*yānēʾṣ*, Hiphil of *nāʾaṣ*); but perhaps we should read here the identical-sounding *yānēṣ*, from *nāṣaṣ*, 'to blossom'. Is the idea that normal food is disgusting, or that (ironically) normal life continues after you die (represented by the almond tree)? Or are both being suggested? A similar question arises about the caperberry: *tāpēr* is from the root *pārar*, 'to break', but the similar-sounding root *pārāh*, 'to blossom', might have been original. It is difficult to decide between these options. See further Fox, *A Time to Tear Down*, 361.

images of the chapter come somewhat into focus. The NIV's 'then' towards the end of the verse obscures the word 'for/because' (*kî*), which shows that the end of verse 5 explains why everything in verses 2–5 has been happening. We are watching as normal life stops for a funeral – a funeral not for 'people' (NIV), but *'ādām*, 'man', an individual – in other words, us. The bell you hear tolling tolls for you.

But this is not a literal description. The sun and moon do not literally go dark during a funeral; people are normally grief-stricken, not afraid; insects do not drag themselves.[22] Qohelet is engaging in a deliberately surreal non-literality to evoke an atmosphere of loss, gloom, decay and dread, which a realistic description would fail to communicate.[23] He is not narrating what literally happens during a funeral, but showing us what a funeral means – our funeral. The images make the coming days of darkness, which we are called to remember in 11:8, salient, vivid, almost palpable. We experience reality shutting down in death. That is the reason both for the confusing imagery and the delay of the information until the end of verse 5 that a funeral is being described.

As we read, wondering exactly what is being described, trying and failing to find referents for the different images, our defences are down and the images can sink into our minds. Once we get to the mourners moving through the streets at the end of verse 5 and the passage clicks into place, it has already done its work. As Fox says, 'The poem retains its power even over those who do not understand it completely – and no one does.'[24] He continues:

---

[22] Fox, *A Time to Tear Down*, 338, 341.

[23] Fox, *A Time to Tear Down*, 338.

[24] Fox, *A Time to Tear Down*, 333. Fox writes that the images evoke something ineffable, a 'total organic response' which resists paraphrase, 339.

Whether we just picture what is happening, or stand back to take in the background as well, or peer closely to resolve the blurry details, we see the same thing: death . . . However we decode the symbols, we will come to the same insights, and the same uneasiness. We finally descry ourselves. We see our own death, and Qohelet will not let us turn away.[25]

Ecclesiastes 12:2–5 is certainly not the only biblical description of death. It is gloriously true that the Christian's death is a departure to be with Christ (Philippians 1:23). It is equally true to say that it is only a kind of falling asleep (1 Kings 2:10), in the hope of the resurrection. But Qohelet's deep love of earthly life, in all its ordinariness, gives him the perspective to see the tragic loss and destruction which each death is. In fact, he portrays it as a loss of cosmic proportions; a number of the images he uses are found most commonly elsewhere in prophetic descriptions of judgment and the Day of the Lord.[26] To be with Christ is far better. But Qohelet helps us see what a massive loss it is each time we bury a body.

The sense of loss continues in verse 6. As above, I do not think we need to decipher exactly what the silver cord and golden bowl mean. Something precious is being destroyed – that is all that is being communicated. The reader should be aware that the 'well' mentioned at the end of the verse is the same word for the 'pit' where the dead go in the Psalms (Psalms 28:1; 30:3; 40:2; 88:5; 143:7). Even here, death casts its shadow.

And so the dust returns to the earth (verse 7). God's curse on Adam in Genesis 3:19 comes true for each one of us. But

---

[25] Fox, *A Time to Tear Down*, 347, 349.
[26] For the darkening of the sun and moon and gathering of storm clouds, compare Ezekiel 32:7–8 and Joel 2:2. Birds of prey appear in Ezekiel 39:4, 17, and the fear in verses 3, 5 can be connected to the fear over Tyre's destruction in Ezekiel 26:17–18.

beautifully, 'the spirit returns to God who gave it' – a reunion with our Creator after the grave, above the sun. Biblical scholars sometimes deny any resurrection hope in the Old Testament until relatively late texts like Daniel 12:2, but Old Testament wisdom literature unambiguously describes embodied life and joy in God's presence after death (for example, Psalm 16:10; Job 19:25–7).[27]

I have argued throughout this commentary that giving too much attention to hope beyond the grave might undermine Qohelet's intention to focus on the uncomfortable realities of life under the sun. But Qohelet's resolute focus on life under the sun is absolutely not a denial of 'above-the-sun' realities. The same God who gave us life and work and the ability to enjoy them (Ecclesiastes 5:17–18, 8:15) does not give them forever. But in his generosity and grace, when he rescinds his gifts, he receives us to himself.

'Vanity of vanities!' (verse 8). Qohelet ends his teaching in exactly the place he began (1:2). The fact that he has learned how to rejoice in life under the sun does not change the basic human condition of brevity and futility. It is also especially appropriate to end with verse 8 after the description of the funeral. Death is the ultimate vanity, the ultimate *hebel*: it unsurpassably represents our brevity, the impermanence and futility of all our (still-good) work. How strange, how absurd, that human beings might reach so high and accomplish so much – only to go into the ground after a few years. 'All is vanity!'

REFLECTION

The best way for readers to reflect on Ecclesiastes 11–12 and apply it is simply to read it unhurriedly. There is no need to repeat here what I have written above about how the text can go

---

[27] Fox denies any idea of resurrection here, taking the verse to speak only of the re-absorption of the life essence into God (*A Time to Tear Down*, 331–2). But this is out of step with Old Testament wisdom literature generally.

to work on a reader who stays open to it. I only wish to draw your attention to an echo between Ecclesiastes 11:7–12:8 and 5:18–20. In that earlier passage, Qohelet said that the one who joyfully receives God's useless gifts of earthly life and work will not much remember the days of his life, because God keeps him occupied with pleasant tasks (verse 20). But in 11:8, Qohelet specifically calls us to remember the coming days of darkness. So which is it? Are we supposed to remember or not?

I think the answer is 'both'. It is very appropriate that we watch and remember the cosmic funeral in chapter 12, listening to the bell tolling for us as the mourners go about in the streets. It is virtually impossible to function in daily life while continually thinking about the grave (our grave, the tombstone engraved with our name). Our Creator knows this. He knows it is good for us to remember the days of darkness – but not all the time. So in his wisdom, he keeps us occupied with pleasant and absorbing work. He would have us live without illusions about what we are really accomplishing in our earthly lives. But he also remembers our dusty frame (Psalm 103:14), and will not crush us continually with unbearable truths.

So keep Ecclesiastes 12 in your Bible reading plan, and let Qohelet imagine with you your own funeral, and all it means. Then turn the page, read other truths, and enjoy this day that God has given to you.

15

Words of Delight: Editor's Conclusion

ECCLESIASTES 12:9–14

The editor recommends Qohelet's teaching to the reader (verses 9–10), while also warning against an excessive love of theorizing (verses 11–12). In light of what Qohelet has taught, humanity's job is basically simple as we await the judgment of all things and the liberation of frustrated creation: to obey God (verses 13–14).

The conclusion of the matter

9 Not only was the Teacher wise, but also he imparted knowledge to the people. He pondered and searched out and set in order many proverbs. **10** The Teacher searched to find just the right words, and what he wrote was upright and true.

11 The words of the wise are like goads, their collected sayings like firmly embedded nails – given by one shepherd.^b **12** Be warned, my son, of anything in addition to them.

Of making many books there is no end, and much study wearies the body.

13 Now all has been heard;
    here is the conclusion of the matter:
fear God and keep his commandments,
    for this is the duty of all mankind.
14 For God will bring every deed into judgment,
    including every hidden thing,
    whether it is good or evil.

---

b 11 Or *Shepherd*

1. Recommendation of Qohelet's wisdom • Ecclesiastes 12:9–10

We considered the relationship between the Teacher Qohelet and the anonymous editor who frames Qohelet's teaching with his own words in the comments on 1:1 above. Since Qohelet has delivered to us everything he has to say about living wisely under the sun, the book's second voice resurfaces to reflect with us on what we have read and to help us evaluate it. This second writer is entirely positive: Qohelet was a sage, but not for himself; his teaching was for the benefit of the people. He laboured long to find words that were (literally) 'words of delight,', morally upright and true (verse 10). Although this may seem a surprising thing to say about Qohelet, it is the earliest recorded 'commentary' on the book, and has the weight of canonical Scripture.

2. The difficulty, divine origin and danger of wisdom • Ecclesiastes 12:11–12

'Words of delight' is, of course, a bit of a surprising thing to say about Qohelet. Even if his wisdom does lead to joy in the face of truths that would provoke many to despair, I doubt that many of us would describe the book this way. But in saying this, the editor is not idealising Qohelet or his wisdom. He admits that wisdom is painful, goading us to go to places we would rather avoid (verse 11). It is as if he sympathises with the reader: 'This has been a tough read.'

Furthermore, this wisdom is given by 'one shepherd'. Elsewhere in Old Testament wisdom texts, God himself is the ultimate source of wisdom (see Proverbs 2:6; Job 28:20–8). Wisdom is more than independent human observation and deduction, and ultimately a source of revelation. This does not lessen wisdom's sometimes painful edge, but does show God himself as our good shepherd, guiding us through Ecclesiastes and our good, useless lives.[1]

The ultimately divine origin of Ecclesiastes and Old Testament wisdom should not, however, lead us to a love of endless reading or a greed for study.[2] More reading (even of other good books) will not equate to more wisdom, for two reasons.[3] First, there will always be more books you have not read and will never have time for – so if you identify wisdom with studying, you will forever be trapped as a beginner. Second, studying is hard, depressing work; overindulge and you will miss out on enjoying life. Qohelet has been at pains to show us how deeply unwise this is. Anything beyond what our One Shepherd has given us should be treated with caution. Endless reading and theorising are a trap.[4]

3. The end of the matter • Ecclesiastes 12:13–14

Given the manifold absurdities of life under the sun, one might think negotiating our lives is a complex matter. But our job is actually simple: fear God and obey him (verse 13). The 'duty of all mankind' (sometimes translated as 'the whole duty of man', ESV) is literally 'this is all of man'. There is nothing else to say about human beings; that is the end of the matter.[5]

---

[1] Eswine, *Recovering Eden*, 229–30.

[2] The phrase is John Owen's, who wisely warned against 'greediness of study' along with worldly ambition and other sins; 'On the Mortification of Sin in Believers', in *The Works of John Owen*, ed. William Goold (reprint; Edinburgh: Banner of Truth, 1905), 6:44.

[3] Packer, *Knowing God*, 94.

[4] Tremper Longman mistranslates this phrase in his commentary, taking it as a warning against Qohelet himself; *Book of Ecclesiastes*, 276, 280–81. See the introduction to this commentary for discussion.

[5] Qohelet never elsewhere uses the common word for 'commandment' which is in this verse (*miṣwāh*). For this and other reasons, some see here a bit of a

If our job is simple, God's is complex: the judgment of every human action in all of history. 'Every hidden thing' means that God's judgment is comprehensive and all-pervasive – nothing is hidden from his sight, and every human being is naked before him. This judgment of course means the punishment of sin and evil, but it also means the positive judgment of each good thing done. This is the way Ecclesiastes speaks of the 'Well done!' given by God to each faithful servant (Matthew 25:21), especially those who accepted God's imposition of frustration and brevity on creation and received and enjoyed earthly life and work as impermanent gifts.

What is beautiful and moving about this final, brief verse is that this judgment of every hidden thing manifestly does not happen in this life – we know all too well from Ecclesiastes itself that judgment sometimes does not seem to happen at all (4:1–3; 8:11, 14). This means that the one book which most insistently draws our attention to the life of this age, under the sun, ends with the spirit returning to God in death (12:7) and receiving God's commendation and reward in the life of the world to come (verse 14). Qohelet has already assured us that God is at work in our work in a beautiful way (11:5–6), but also assured us that we would never see how (8:16–17). We are given a bit more of a hint here: the earthly work and lives that God gave us, from which we got nothing permanent while we lived under the sun, will one day receive a very great reward. In this way, Ecclesiastes stands in harmony with those great New Testament texts that speak of standing before the judgment seat of God and receiving our 'above-the-sun' reward (compare 2 Corinthians 5:10).

---

pushback against Qohelet, as if the author were qualifying his commendation of the book: 'Yes, take Qohelet's wisdom to heart, but remember also to obey!' But since Qohelet repeatedly has told us to fear God (3:14; 5:7; 7:18; 8:12–13), it is difficult for me to see any tension with this verse and the rest of Ecclesiastes.

Because of this, we can labour and minister now in ignorant hope, eagerly awaiting that day when the sun falls from the heavens (2 Peter 3:10), creation is made new, and our great Savior comes to reward those who once laboured in vain but will then enter into the joy of their master (Matthew 25:21).[6]

REFLECTION

Throughout this commentary, I have more than once asked the reader to imagine the unpleasant realities of the brevity and vanity of life under the sun. For the book's final passage, however, it is appropriate to ask you to imagine something unimaginable – something that may even be dangerous to try to imagine, so narrow and earthbound are our expectations, so easy it is for us to misapprehend the resurrection life which awaits us. But I think, at this particular junction, it is still appropriate. (Please take all of this as a guess, a suggestion, meant to inspire joyful endurance in our certain reward, not certainty about the details.)

I want you to imagine the sun falling from the sky.

As best you can, imagine not just your death, but the end of this age, as the elements are destroyed with fire (2 Peter 3:10) and we are ushered into that eternal kingdom (2 Peter 1:11).

You come to yourself and realise you are lying on the ground. You sit up; grass of vibrant green is beneath you, sifted by a scented breeze. The air is lit up with a crystal, singing shimmer. You take a deep breath and stand up; you feel unexpectedly well, far better than when you were lying in that hospital bed, waiting for the end. You realise you are surrounded by others, and with a start, you recognise the faces: they are not worn with wrinkles and heavy with care, as you remember, but with their very essences shining through; all the people you lived and worked and went

---

[6] Eric Ortlund, 'Labouring in Hopeless Hope: Encouragement for Christians from Ecclesiastes', *Themelios* 39 (2014): 289.

to church with. Each one is lit up with a light and a joy you have never seen before and they each finally, really look like themselves. You embrace each one, especially those you missed so painfully, whom death took from you too soon. Even those who hurt and wronged you hurry to beg your forgiveness. You quiet them and smile, and it is joy itself to forgive them. Many other saints stand around you, each a living, distinct image of the joy of their master; but then they all stand aside.

A man is walking towards you. You have never seen him before, but you recognise him. How could you not recognise him? You fall to your knees.

Jesus, the Lord Christ himself, pulls you up and embraces you, and the very voice that spoke Aramaic so many years ago speaks your name. 'My child, my brother, my sister, I am so glad you are here. I could not bear to start the new age until you were with us. Put your finger in my wrists and my side – do you see the marks of my love for you? I was so happy to go through that torture, because it meant I got you.'

'But Lord, so many times . . . I failed you so many times . . .'

'Hush. I was happy to suffer that so that you wouldn't have to. We will never speak of it again. Now: you were faithful to me in your life and you stuck with what I called you to do, even when it did not make sense, even when no one else saw or thanked you, even when they criticised you for obeying me, and even though it all turned to dust. Well done, oh, well done, my good and faithful servant!'

And heaven itself will thunder in acclamation and tribute – every angel will sing, and the crystal sea will crash and roar, and every saint who ever lived will shout and cheer, all for you. And perhaps best of all, you will be able to receive Christ's praise with simple joy. There will be no awkward self-consciousness.

And Jesus will take you by the hand and say, 'You never saw how, but I was at work in all your work. Let me show you what I accomplished through you. Let me show you what your life, what all those days of labour, really meant. Come, enter my joy.'

And although you thought yourself at the point of bursting for sheer happiness, you will feel at those words your own capacity for limitless joy expand as the great symphony begins, and your earthly life forms part of the melody in a way you never expected – as real life begins, the best story you have ever read, and you are one thread in the narrative, and each chapter grows better than the last. 'God will bring every deed into judgment, including every hidden thing.'